THE *Invisible* HEART

THE MIT PRESS
CAMBRIDGE, MASSACHUSETTS
LONDON, ENGLAND

THE *Invisible* HEART

AN ECONOMIC ROMANCE

RUSSELL ROBERTS

Library of Congress Cataloging-in-Publication Data

Roberts, Russell.
  The invisible heart : an economic romance / Russell Roberts.
    p.   cm.
  Includes bibliographical references.
  ISBN 0-262-18210-6 (hc. : alk. paper)
  1. Economics—Fiction. I. Title.
HB171 .R617   2001
813'.6—dc21   00-055402

Author's Note: The Edwards School, its students and employees and their friends and family, the conglomerate HealthNet and its employees and their families, the Office of Corporate Responsibility and its employees, the members of Congress, and the employees of various government agencies described here are products of the author's imagination. Any resemblance to real folk, real companies, real schools, real politicians, or real bureaucrats is purely coincidental. All of the other companies and people mentioned here are real. I have tried to portray them and the American economy as accurately as possible. Sources can be found at the back of the book.

Lyrics from "When Numbers Get Serious" cited on page 89, © 1983 Paul Simon. Used by permission of the publisher: Paul Simon Music.

For Sharon

CONTENTS

ACKNOWLEDGMENTS

Many, many people gave me help in writing this book, ranging from general encouragement to detailed comments on various drafts of the manuscript. Their views are all over the political and philosophical spectrum. Many of them disagree with some or many of the ideas in the book. Some agree with almost all of them. Any errors that remain are mine.

I have been lucky to learn from great teachers, great students, and great books. Some of the latter you can find in the section on further reading. Among my many teachers, I wish particularly to thank Gary Becker, Milton Friedman, Deirdre McCloskey, Sol Polachek, George Stigler, and Ken Wertz. They were instrumental in making me passionate about the economic way of thinking.

This book got rejected a lot in its early and late incarnations. I am grateful to Victoria Richardson Warneck, Mina Cerny Kumar, and Jane Macdonald for their help and enthusiasm, Judy Feldmann for her comments and excellent editing, and all the people at MIT Press for their support.

I am grateful to be able to work at the Center for the Study of American Business and to be part of Washington

University in St. Louis. The founder and director of the Center, Murray Weidenbaum, has created a wonderful environment for thinking and writing.

For encouragement, ideas, support, and helpful comments on early drafts I wish to thank Derek Blakeley, Yael Bloom, Catherine Bradford, Anna Cantwell, Les Cook, Morgan Fahey-Vornberg, Tamar Fredman, Larry and Phyllis Terry Friedman, William Frucht, Pete Geddes, Susan Ginsburg, Dan Gressel, Lisa Harris, Jamie Harris-Gershon, Jon Hart, David Henderson, Scott Jennings, Kevin Kane, Robert Kirk, David Kowalczyk, Barbara and David Kupfer, Jennifer Krupp, Marc Law, Dwight Lee, Michael Levin, Arthur Lieber's Metro Class, Gordon MacKenzie, Dick Mahoney, Allan Mazur, Chris Moseley, Stephen Moss, Peter Mueser, Alan Nemes, Rafi Nemes, Bruce Nichols, Robin Orvis, Ed Peets, Sarah Pierson, Dan Pink, Kathryn Ratté, Andrea Millen Rich, Jennifer and Joe Roberts, Max Rosenthal, Andy Rutten, Allen Sanderson, Hyim Shafner, and Sara Winkelman, Dalit Sharfman, Murray Weidenbaum, and Ellianna Yolkut.

Special thanks go to: my parents Shirley and Ted Roberts for inspiration, poetry, heart, and a passion to change the world. They also read the manuscript many times and gave wonderful feedback; to Mindee and Zev Fredman for Sinatra advice, excellent feedback on earlier drafts, and many hours of discussion about the topics here and how best to repair the world; to Bevis and Patience

Schock for many great suggestions and hours of conversation on the topics here; to Don Boudreaux for great comments on early drafts and hours of conversation on how to communicate good economics clearly; and to Gary Belsky who pushed me to make the book better, gave extraordinary advice on improving the language, and who, outside of immediate family members, set the record for multiple readings of the manuscript.

I want to thank my children for always asking "What's happening with Sam and Laura?" and for listening enthusiastically to the answer.

Finally, I want to thank my wife Sharon who never tired of reading draft after draft and improving each with her comments and who patiently provided help and inspiration through the five years this book evolved with all the ups and downs. She knows more about the invisible heart than anyone.

Every individual . . . neither intends to promote the public interest, nor knows how much he is promoting it . . . he intends only his own gain, and he is in this, as in many other cases, led by an invisible hand to promote an end which was no part of his intention.

ADAM SMITH
An Inquiry into the Nature and Causes of The Wealth of Nations

There is only one difference between a bad economist and a good one: the bad economist confines himself to the visible effect; the good economist takes into account both the effect that can be seen and those effects that must be foreseen.

FREDERIC BASTIAT
"What Is Seen and What Is Not Seen"
Selected Essays in Political Economy

You gotta have heart.

RICHARD ADLER AND JERRY ROSS
Damn Yankees

One OPENING DAY

The students looked up from their conversations as Sam Gordon entered the classroom. He was tall and lanky. His walk was the unfolding of a marionette, all knees and elbows swinging briskly as he hurried into the room. His dark curly hair brought out the paleness of his skin. He wore khaki pants with a jacket and tie. The tie was a once-a-year ritual for the first day of class.

Before speaking, Sam looked heavenward. By the end of the year, having seen him look up so many times, his students assumed that the answers to all the questions in economics must be inscribed on the ceilings of the Edwards School. But Sam was only gathering his thoughts.

Sam wrote his name on the board, took a deep breath to still the butterflies, pushed his wire-rims up on the bridge of his nose and turned to face his students.

"My name is Sam Gordon. And this is Life Skills 101," he said.

A student giggled.

"Actually, this is the senior elective, 'The World of Economics.' There is no prerequisite for this class other than an exceedingly open mind. Quiz time!" Sam suddenly announced with delight. "Take out a piece of paper and put your name at the top."

A few quiet groans rose up from the students.

"I know," Sam said. "First day of class, senior year of high school, and already a quiz. Don't worry. It's easy."

He went to the board and wrote down two numbers: 531,000,000,000 and 16,500,000,000.

"The first number, 531 billion, is the amount of crude oil, measured in barrels, that's still under the ground. They're called reserves. The second number is the world's annual consumption of crude oil. Here's the quiz: when will the world run out of oil? You have one minute."

"One minute?" a protester blurted out. "Can we use a calculator?" asked another.

"Yes," Sam said.

"Do you want it in days or years or hours or minutes?" asked another.

"That's up to you."

As the students pounded on their calculators, Sam looked peacefully around the room. The Edwards School was a beautiful place to teach—richly patterned, full-grained oak everywhere, from the door frame to the crown molding to the desks arrayed in neat rows. Sam felt the sweet ache of nerves and anticipation that marks the first day of a new school year.

There were 18 kids in the class. A tall blond-haired girl slouched in the third row, staring off into the distance, refusing, it appeared, to even try the quiz. The others continued to scribble feverishly and work their calculator keys. "Ten seconds!" Sam announced. More groans.

"Time's up. Circle your best guess, please." Sam walked down the rows, picking up their papers. He leafed through them as he made his way back to the front of the room.

"What's your name?" Sam asked, stopping in front of the blond girl in the third row.

"Amy."

"Amy, what was your answer?"

"I left it blank. I think it was a trick question."

"Ahh. And why is that, Amy?"

"Because this is an economics class, not a class on how to use a calculator. Or a calendar."

"So what's the trick?"

"I don't know. I don't know enough economics to figure it out, but I'm still thinking."

"Thinking is the goal of this course," Sam said, moving to the front of the class. "Be skeptical. Think for yourself. And remember a few core principles of human behavior. Learn how to use them and you will excel in this class. The right answer is that we will never run out of oil."

Sam stopped and let his words sink in. A student in the last row turned to his neighbor and whispered, "What kind of answer is that? This guy's crazy!"

A lot of people thought Sam Gordon was crazy, but few people knew him well. Birds of a feather flock together. Being a strange bird, Sam was part of a very small flock. Later in the year, when his troubles would begin, no one would know the real story. The rumors that filled the halls were only guesswork.

It was surprising that a school as staid as the Edwards School had hired him in the first place. Perhaps the most prestigious private high school in the nation's capital, the Edwards School was tucked into a quiet residential neighborhood in the northwest quadrant of the city, a few blocks from the Washington National Cathedral and the Zoo. In the early days of the school, in the early part of the twentieth century, the teachers often exploited this proximity to remind students that man lay poised between the angels and the animals, the divine and the profane; it was the job of the Edwards School to push man in the right direction. In modern times, the school was merely content to push young men and women northward, in the direction of the Ivy League colleges.

The Edwards School hired Sam because he had a master's degree in economics and four years of previous teaching experience. He had turned thirty the previous summer. In his first year at the school, he had taught a couple of sections of the advanced placement course in economics along with a class on government and politics. This year he had added his first elective, "The

World of Economics," where he had free rein to teach whatever he wanted.

"Think, think, think!" Sam was telling the class. "There is a finite amount of crude oil in the world. We use immense amounts of it every day. Obviously, we'll run out of oil some day. Won't we?"

Sam paused and looked out at the rows of faces. Would anyone answer?

"Well, it *appears* we'll run out of oil," said Amy.

"Amy, do you like pistachio nuts?" Sam asked her.

"Doesn't everyone?"

"Suppose for your birthday I gave you a room full of pistachio nuts in the shell. It's a big room, say the size of this classroom. The room is filled with pistachio nuts up to a height of five feet. There are millions of them. Happy birthday, Amy. Welcome to the Nut Room. The nuts in this room are yours for the taking. Any time you want to come in here and help yourself, there is no charge. Bring your friends if you'd like. Just wade in and have a pistachio party. You're thrilled of course—"

"Thrilled?"

"OK, mildly happy. Work with me." Sam said, smiling. "You're happy because you love pistachio nuts. Outside the Nut Room, they're expensive. Inside, they're free. There's only one rule in the Nut Room. As you eat the nuts, you've got to leave the shells in the room. You can't take them out with you. At first, that's no problem. For the first few days and maybe weeks and months, the pistachios are plentiful. But as the years go by, it takes longer and longer to find a pistachio. The shells start getting in the way. You come in with your friends and you spend hours wading through the shells of pistachios you've already eaten in order to find one containing a nut. Your friends say, we've got to stop meeting like this. 'Why?' you ask. 'Don't you like free pistachio nuts?' And what do your friends say in response?"

"The nuts aren't free any more," Amy said.

"Exactly!" Sam shouted in triumph. "After a while, you're better off paying for nuts in the store rather than spending hours trying to extract a nut from the depths of the pile. The cost of the nuts in the Nut Room has gotten too high. It's the same with oil. Years before the last drop of oil is found and extracted, we'll walk away from oil as an energy source. It will be too hard to find new reserves. Or too expensive to extract the reserves we know about. Long before we run out of oil, we'll switch to cheaper alternatives. Remember the pistachios!"

The kid in the back row leaned over again to his friend. "I told you he was crazy. Too much time in the Nut Room."

><

Down the hall from Sam's classroom, Laura Silver tried to calm her nerves. While Sam Gordon had butterflies at the beginning of his class, Laura Silver felt something more sizable, perhaps bats, flapping away at her insides. Teaching at the Edwards School was her first real job. She wrote her name on the board, and the class, English Literature.

"I'm Ms. Silver. This is English Literature. And our first assignment will be to read *Great Expectations* by Charles Dickens."

Laura looked up from her notes. Expressionless as fish, the class waited for Laura to continue. She wore a long patterned skirt and a ribbed top. Her cascade of auburn hair was held back from her face with a black hair-band. She wore no make-up. She went to the board and wrote, "Getting and spending, we lay waste our powers."

"Does anyone know who said that?"

"Shakespeare?" someone ventured.

"Always a good guess. Then try Alexander Pope or the Bible. But this quote's from a poem by William Wordsworth. Before we talk about it, let's move these desks into a circle so we can talk."

The physical task brought the class to life. When the fifteen desks were in place, Laura added her chair to the group. She then walked around the circle and had the students introduce themselves and mention a favorite book.

"Now," Laura said when they had finished, "I'd like you to take out a piece of paper and try to put in your own words what you think Wordsworth is trying to say. There is no right or wrong answer. Just do the best you can and then we'll talk about it."

Laura was lucky to be teaching at the Edwards School. She was only twenty-four. She had majored in English at Yale and had spent the past year on a kibbutz in Israel, picking fruit and working in a box factory, then stopping off in Italy for the summer to explore Florence and improve her Italian. It was unusual for the Edwards School to hire someone with no experience. But her letters of recommendation from her college professors had been raves and her guest lecture on Dickens to a twelfth grade elective at the school had clinched her appointment.

She planned on teaching at the Edwards School for two years. Then it was off to law school. Law school seemed as inevitable as growing up. Both her parents were lawyers. She loved to argue. She wanted to do her part in repairing the world.

"OK," Laura said, after a few minutes had passed. "The poet

says, 'Getting and spending, we lay waste our powers.' What do you think he meant by getting and spending? Getting and spending what?"

The first day of class is always like a blind date. It is particularly hard when a first-time teacher faces ninth graders who are new to the school. Laura's question hung in the air for a moment. Then, to her relief, a girl directly across from her raised her hand.

"Emily?"

"Getting and spending money?"

"And why do you say that?"

"You spend it. What else could it be?"

"So please read us your version of what Wordsworth is trying to say."

"Earning and spending money weakens a person."

"Excellent. That makes a lot of sense. But it raises a question. Why did Wordsworth say 'getting' instead of 'earning'?" Laura looked around the circle expectantly. A hand went up.

"Steven?"

"I think Wordsworth wanted to use the word 'getting' because it doesn't sound as nice as earning. Earning money seems like a good thing. Getting money doesn't seem as nice."

"That's an interesting thought. Why do you find 'getting' to be less attractive than 'earning'?"

"Well, you can 'get' money in lots of ways besides earning it. Earning money sounds honest and fair. Getting it sounds a little bit, I don't know, grubby. Like stealing. Or tricking somebody out of their money."

"Does anyone agree or disagree with that? Yes, Kim?"

"I think Wordsworth was trying to say that it's all the same.

That earning and stealing and, like, the whole money thing has a nastiness about it."

"Very good." Laura said, smiling in encouragement, "What did you write for your interpretation of the quote?"

><

Down the hall, Sam was pacing back and forth, eyeing the class mischievously. He took a dollar bill from his pocket and put it on his desk.

"Let's play a game," he said, his eyes full of mischief. "The first person who gets this dollar bill can have it."

The strangeness of the situation froze the students for a moment. Then a student in the second row bolted out of his seat and grabbed the dollar.

"Well done!" Sam exulted, coming over to the boy and shaking his hand. The boy smiled sheepishly. Sam returned to the desk. He took out a five-dollar bill from his pocket. He showed it to the class, then let it flutter to the desktop.

"Same game," he said calmly.

The class exploded into motion. There was a din of chairs scraping, bodies hurtling forward. There was a brief tussle, then a shout of triumph. Sam again shook the hand of the student who had survived the struggle.

"Exciting, isn't it?" Sam said, turning to the class. "Money on the table is a great motivator." The students who had sprung forward returned to their seats. Some lingered by the desk for a moment in hopes of another round.

Sam waited until they were seated, then leaped onto his desk. He took a twenty-dollar bill from his pocket and dangled it over the heads of the students, holding it gingerly between his thumb and forefinger. A good portion of the class surged forward, laughing and shouting, jostling for position, heads tilted upward, arms outstretched.

"Just kidding," Sam said, putting the bill back in his pocket. "I like teaching you economics, but twenty dollars is too expensive a lesson. Can you believe that some people actually think that economics is boring?" Sam marveled from atop the desk, towering over the class. "Now tell me. What is the lesson of this game?" he asked.

><

"Materialism corrupts us," Kim answered in response to Laura's request for her paraphrase of Wordsworth.

"That's very nice. And very efficient. A mere three words."

"It's OK." Kim answered. "But it doesn't have the majesty of 'getting and spending, we lay waste our powers.' I think that's why he left off the word 'money.'"

"Why's that?"

"'Getting and spending *money*, we lay waste our powers,'" Kim recited, wrinkling her nose. "Adding the word 'money' ruins the rhythm of the line. It doesn't sing. You know what I mean?"

Laura smiled. She wanted to hug Kim but she managed to restrain herself. She looked around the circle. "OK, let's look at the last part of the line. Do you think Wordsworth is saying more than just materialism *corrupts* us? What does it mean to 'lay waste our powers'? Sounds pretty devastating, doesn't it?"

><

"By the way," Sam was saying, "that 531 billion barrels of reserves and the 16.5 billion barrels of consumption were actually for *1970*. If nothing else had changed, we should have run out of oil around thirty years later. But by the time the year 2000 actually rolled around somehow reserves had somehow climbed to a *trillion* barrels even though the world was using about 26 billion barrels annually. We suddenly had almost forty years worth of consumption left."

"How could that be?" a student asked.

"Self-interest. When the price of oil jumped up later in the '70s, consumers found ways to use oil more efficiently and producers found new reserves. So we're even farther away from running out of oil than we were in 1970. Never underestimate the power of self-interest. You see this tie?" Sam said, pointing to his neckwear. "The profile on this tie is Adam Smith, probably the most famous economist of all time. He understood the power of self-interest as well as anyone." The bell rang, announcing the end of class.

><

Relief washed over Laura. Her mother had been right: forty-five minutes was not very long. She gave the class their first reading assignment in *Great Expectations*.

"Ms. Silver?" a student asked.

"Yes."

"I thought we were going to be reading *Great Expectations* by Dickens. Why did we start the class with a quote from Wordsworth?"

"Good question," Laura said, pleased that someone had noticed. "Start reading *Great Expectations* and you'll find the answer."

><

Word of Sam's game of "money on the table" spread quickly through the school that afternoon. Laura wondered what a character like Sam Gordon would think of Wordsworth. In fact, she wondered if many economists had even *heard* of Wordsworth. On her way out of school, she stopped by Sam's classroom and peered in.

He was gone. Laura wandered in and looked around. She loved the sweet space of an empty classroom. In college, when studying for an exam, she always preferred the solitude of an empty classroom to the tumult of the library. Here, the black-and-white portraits of dead economists that Sam had chosen for his classroom decor took the joy out of the room. They were a dreary-looking lot. Maybe the mere study of "getting and spending" could lay waste one's powers.

As she turned to leave, a splash of color in the corner caught her eye. It was a poster for the movie *It's a Wonderful Life.* Jimmy Stewart held Donna Reed in his arms forever. Seeing such romance next to all of these dead men in black-and-white was like watching someone flirt at a funeral.

Laura looked over at the desk at the front of the class where Sam had stood dropping dollar bills into the grasping hands of his students. How could a man reward greed, yet honor a movie dedicated to the principle of people before profits?

Two BEAUTY AND THE BEAST

The car hugs the curve of the road like a speed skater taking a corner. The man at the wheel, who looks younger than his fifty years, likes the feeling of control. The Virginia pine forest flashes by and the sunlight, coming just over the horizon, darts in and out of the spaces between the branches, dappling the hood of the BMW with patches of deeper silver here, a flash of light there.

Frank Sinatra's voice singing "My Way" fills the space of the car so completely that you wonder if there is room for the man's thoughts. At the final verse, the man raises the volume a notch and savors the voice, world-weary yet triumphant.

∞

Thirty miles to the north, in Washington, D.C., a woman pounds away on a stair-stepper in a health club. Her headphones weave the harmonies of the Indigo Girls through her thoughts. But it is hard to imagine that she is thinking of little else beyond the driving and pumping of her arms and legs. Her red hair is pulled back tightly in a ponytail to keep it out of her eyes. Without stopping, she towels the sweat from her face and neck and redoubles her efforts as she finishes the workout. Soon she is showered and dressed, striding through the front door, headed for the Dupont Circle Metro stop, wading through the swarm as the sidewalk comes to life with people hurrying to work.

∞

Back in the Virginia countryside, the man rolls the car into the parking spot labeled "Charles Krauss, CEO." The building is all chrome and glass, corners jutting out at odd angles, giving the building a jagged look, as if it had been thrust upward from below the ground or hewn from some massive rock hidden in the heart of the forest. The company name, HEALTHNET, is a deep metallic blue embedded in one of the facets in the front.

Krauss takes the steps two at a time and glides through the front door, past the security guard behind the imposing desk who greets him by name. Heading for his office, he is pleased to see the corridors busy with early arrivals. A steady chorus of greetings accompanies him. He hardly notices. His mind is busy churning through the day's agenda.

∞

On a street corner in Washington, D.C., the Metro's escalator coughs up a steady stream of workers who scurry under the looming dome of the Capitol. The woman is swept along with the crowd and after a short walk, climbs the gray concrete steps of a standard-issue Washington government office building. There is a brief wait as the security guard rummages through the briefcase of a visitor ahead of her. Then she walks through the metal detector and heads down a dingy corridor. She turns a corner; another long corridor and then a glass door—stenciled in white on the door it says: OFFICE OF CORPORATE RESPONSIBILITY, and just below it, ERICA BALDWIN, DIRECTOR.

On the other side of the door there is light and activity. Workers are setting up brightly colored partitions, creating new office space. The receptionist greets her with "Good morning, Erica." She heads to the corner office.

∞

To the south, Charles Krauss reaches the executive suite. The receptionist at the entrance to the suite looks up briefly to greet him with a brisk "Good morning, sir." She hands him a cup of coffee and a sheaf of papers. He smiles, grabs them without stopping and enters the office, a sanctuary of steel, chrome, black marble, and leather. He turns on his laptop and a spreadsheet comes up, a green labyrinth of cells and numbers. His hands fly across the keys.

∞

As Erica Baldwin enters her office, the phone is already ringing. "Erica Baldwin," she says, as she takes out her schedule for the day, cradling the phone on her shoulder. She settles into her chair, and with her free hand reaches for a yellow legal pad. If she listens hard enough, she can still hear the fading rhythms of the Indigo Girls ringing in the air.

Three DANGER AND DELIGHT

"Spare change? Have a good day. Spare change? Have a good day. Spare change? Thank you, sir. Have a good day. Spare change?"

The man sat on the ground near the entrance to the Woodley Park Metro station. His clothes were filthy, his hair matted to his head. The sun was out and the temperature was in the upper 50s—

a mild November day in Washington, D.C. Still, the man wore a heavy wool overcoat, its pockets stuffed with plastic bags and other keepsakes. He was known as Fast Eddie. No one knew why or even if his name was really Eddie. A regular at the Woodley Park station, he was known for his unfailing politeness.

"Spare change?"

Fast Eddie looked up from his mantra to see a tall young man in wire-rim glasses stop in front of him and block the sunlight. Sam Gordon reached into his pocket and pulled out two quarters and a dime.

"How are you today, Fast Eddie?"

"Doing fine, sir. Doing fine. Rain gonna come if the sun don't shine."

"Right as always. Stay dry."

"Thank you, sir."

Sam turned away and bumped into a young woman passing by.

"Excuse me," he said. "I'm very sorry."

The woman looked at him, looked away, then looked again.

"Don't you work at the Edwards School?" she asked.

"Yes."

"I'm Laura Silver from the English Department," she said, extending her hand. "I've seen you at faculty meetings."

"Sam Gordon. Economics."

The young woman flashed a quick smile of recognition. So this was the man who put the money on the table.

"So how do you manage to pay your rent?"

"Excuse me?"

"You seem to specialize in giving away money. I heard you give money to your students. And now this guy—"

chapter three

"Fast Eddie? I don't do much for him. Just a few coins and a smile."

"Don't you worry that he's going to waste it on drugs and alcohol?"

Sam was about to start the little tango step necessary to get on the escalator. He stopped and turned toward Laura.

"Given his situation, I'm not sure I'd call it a waste. He looks like he needs a drink."

Laura looked into Sam's eyes. Surely he was teasing her. But his face was calm and free of laughter. He was waiting for her reply. Laura wasn't sure she could have a civil conversation with someone who thought poisoning the homeless was a gesture of compassion. But this cheerful evasion of responsibility was so annoying and wrong she had to respond.

"Look, Sam, I hope it won't offend you, but—"

"Very little offends me. Disagreement *never* offends me."

Laura looked back over her shoulder at Fast Eddie, sitting cross-legged on the ground, his hand outstretched.

"I just don't see how it helps to give alcohol to an alcoholic or cocaine to a drug addict," she said. "It's like giving a sick person a more intense dose of the disease. My brother Andrew carries little cans of V-8 juice in his briefcase. When beggars ask him for money, he gives them one. That way he knows he's not adding to their problems."

Sam could see that Laura was very proud of her brother. "What's he do for a living?" he asked.

"He's a lawyer for the Consumer Product Safety Commission."

Sam was not a big fan of the Consumer Product Safety Commission but there was no need to alienate someone he had just met. He could always use another friend at the Edwards School. He said nothing.

"Isn't that a great idea?" Laura asked.

"The Consumer Product Safety Commission?" Sam asked. Was she going to ferret out his true feelings?

"No. Carrying around little V-8 juices."

"I don't know. I doubt the beggar cares about getting his minimum daily requirement of vitamins. His life stinks. He wants to get high. He tries to sell the V-8 juice on the street. If he's successful, your brother has inconvenienced the beggar and had no nutritional impact. If the beggar can't sell the can, he drinks it, takes the money he would have spent on lunch and uses it to buy crack or liquor. So did your well-intentioned brother participate in the beggar's habit, or are his hands clean?"

They eased their way on to the escalator. Laura's mind wandered for a moment. The escalators of the D.C. Metro go on forever. They always made her think of a scene from some Italian film, where the ride downward would be a surreal symbol for a trip into hell and the upward journey a passage to redemption. Sam's mind wandered as well. But he thought of the taxes necessary to dig so deep.

"When you give to charity," Laura said, "it seems to me you have a right to give it as you see fit."

"I agree. It's your money. Or your brother's. But a person who gives away V-8 juice instead of money is being charitable in a selfish way."

Laura nearly winced at hearing Andrew described as selfish.

"I think," Sam continued, "you should try to help people on their terms, not your own. People use the same argument when they talk about motorcycle helmets."

"I hope you're not against helmet laws. The next thing you'll tell me is you're against laws that require people to wear seat belts."

Laura laughed in anticipation of Sam's response.

"I'm against both of those laws," Sam said.

"But seat belts save lives!" Laura said in exasperation.

"I like saving lives, but that's not the only goal of life. If it were, you would move away from Washington D.C. to a safer city. You would never ride in a car. You would stop eating ice cream. The goal of life is to live as richly as you can—"

"You say that because you're an economist," Laura interrupted.

"I don't mean living richly in the sense of having a lot of money. I mean the sense of fully experiencing everything that makes us human. If people want to risk their lives by not wearing a seat belt in exchange for greater comfort, or to save money by buying a less expensive car without air bags, then I think they should have that right."

"But they don't realize that the discomfort of a seat belt or the cost of an air bag is worth it. They just assume that an accident is never going to happen."

"I don't know," Sam said pensively. "Maybe they *do* know and they just feel differently about the costs and benefits. It reminds me of this dinner party. I was sitting across the table from a doctor who worked in the emergency room at a local hospital. He was in favor of mandatory air bags for the same reason that you're in favor of seat belts. He told me they save lives. But they're expensive, I reminded him. Perhaps to some people their cost is not worth the safety."

"But how could the cost not be worth the extra safety?"

"Ahhhhhh," Sam sighed. "A profound question. There is no free lunch. More safety means less of something else. Force people to buy safety devices for their cars and maybe their kids don't go to college or get music lessons."

"If the kid is killed in a car wreck it won't matter."

"Quite right. And now we know that even air bags can kill kids. But ignore that. Let's assume that all air bags work perfectly."

"OK."

"Air bags or seat belts aren't the only way to keep a kid safe in a car. There are other, cheaper ways. You can drive more slowly. You can drive less often. You can postpone travel when it rains. It's better to give the parents the choice than to force them to create safety in a particular way. It is hard to believe, but you don't want to have the safest possible car."

"That's ridiculous."

"Maybe it is. But it's the way I look at the world. I'm not saying safety is bad. Safety is great. I'm saying that it's possible for safety to get too expensive. Here's an easy way to see it. The safest car is no car at all. That's the only way to guarantee that you don't get into a car accident. Most of us understand that no car at all is too much safety."

"That's a lovely theory. But what if people make the wrong choices—what if they're not as knowledgeable or informed as we are? They'll make the wrong choices. They won't be safe enough for their own good."

"I wonder how you'd feel if someone who claims to be better informed than you are stopped you from eating beef or from going skiing or from living in a particular neighborhood because he,

Mr. Knows-better-than-you-do, thinks the risks from those activities are too high. Do you think his education and good intentions would win you over?"

"Maybe. Maybe not. It wouldn't hurt me to at least consider stopping those activities."

"Oh no. You don't have a choice. I'm all in favor of worriers providing the less-worried among us with more information at their own expense, out of the goodness of their hearts. But we're talking about foreclosing people's choices against their will."

"I thought you were allowed to turn off your air bag."

"Deactivating it is against the law. In theory, you're allowed to install an on-off switch. You have to write a letter to an official in Washington explaining why you want to turn it off, say because your mother drives your car sometimes and she's only 5′ tall and prone to being killed if the air bag deploys. If the official finds your reason acceptable, he sends you a letter giving you permission to turn it off. Isn't that thoughtful? He sends you a letter giving you permission to use your own car as you see fit. Then all you have to do is find a mechanic willing to put in the switch. He has to hope you won't sue him if someone is hurt or killed. If he's willing to do it, you're out about $500. So it's not really voluntary."

"I guess you're right."

"Anyway, this doctor at this dinner party got on his high horse, the one that helps him look down on economists and other lower life-forms, and told me that if I worked in the emergency room like he did and saw what people looked like after a car wreck at sixty miles an hour, I'd agree with him."

"What did you say?"

"I went a little berserk. 'Do you really think people don't know what happens to their body when it hits a windshield at sixty miles per hour? Do you think it's a secret only revealed to doctors and people in driver's ed. and traffic school who watch those gory movies to deter drunk driving? We know, doctor, we know. Maybe some people don't wear their seat belts because their values of the costs and benefits are not the same as yours.'"

"What did he say to that?"

"I didn't give him a chance to reply. I asked him if his car had an air bag. Just a stab in the dark really. But I hit home. His car did not have an air bag. He said that at the time he was looking for a car, only Chrysler and Mercedes offered air bags as an option and he didn't like them. Here was a guy who chose style over safety. But he still wanted to deny that choice to others. I'll never understand a person like that."

"You'll probably never understand me, then." Laura said cheerfully. "I think wearing a seat belt is a good idea."

"I think the world of seat belts myself. That's why I wear mine whenever I drive."

Laura wasn't sure how to react to Sam. His perspective on the world turned a wait for a subway train into an intellectual tennis match. And it always seemed to be his serve. She was relieved when the train arrived. It was crowded and Sam and Laura found themselves pushed close together, swaying gently back and forth as the train started forward.

For a moment, Sam let go of the bar he was holding to clean his glasses. Laura took a good look at him as he used the slack in his shirt to buff the lenses. He reminded her of a blackboard filled with equations, chalk dust everywhere. His intensity brought out her own passion. She felt like she was back in her dorm at Yale, arguing some philosophical point late into the night.

"Let me get this straight," Laura said. "You wear a seat belt but you don't want to force people to protect themselves. What's the harm in helping people?"

"Maybe not a lot with any one law like mandatory seat belts. But the more you limit people's choices, even in the name of helping them, the more responsibility you take away from them. I don't like it when people make decisions for me and I believe in extending the same courtesy to others."

"But are you comfortable knowing that people will often make mistakes?" Laura asked.

"I am. I probably think they make fewer mistakes than you think they do. But life is about choices and taking responsibility. It's about learning from those mistakes and growing up. When my folks first got married, they bought a house in University City, Missouri, just outside of the city limits of St. Louis. The house was built around the time of the 1904 World's Fair. It was a beautiful old house with creaky wood floors and two fireplaces. It would be the house I would grow up in. But even though my dad and the owner agreed to a deal, there was still a problem."

The train stopped and disgorged half its riders. Laura and Sam were able to find seats next to each other.

"When the house changed owners," Sam continued, "it had to comply with the new housing code. There was a front porch that ran the width of the house. It was lovely. According to the housing code, a porch that was three feet or more off the ground was required to have a railing. Ours was four. So we had to have a railing if we wanted to move in."

"Was it such a big deal to put up a railing?"

"Two people were very upset. The first was the previous owner. He had rehabbed the house to make sure that it looked as close as possible to how it had looked in 1906 when it was built. He had a photograph of the house from the turn of the century. No railing. The second person who was very upset was my dad."

"He probably didn't want to pay for the railing."

"Actually, he didn't care about the money. When my dad signed the deal, the seller agreed to pay for the new railing if the city forced them to put one up. No, my dad was upset for a different reason. He liked the idea of having a slightly dangerous porch."

"The apple doesn't fall far from the tree," Laura interjected. "I wonder if there's a gene for weirdness."

Sam smiled. "I'll take that as a compliment," he said. "Anyway, my dad and the seller went to the hearing to request a waiver on historical grounds. The seller waxed poetic about historical authenticity and got nowhere. The head of the Board of Aldermen kept saying that he had a responsibility to the children who would play on that porch. My dad explained that he had no children. And the alderman countered that he might have children in the future, which of course turned out to be true. The alderman was worried about those children and any others who might visit the house."

"Fair enough."

"Sure. But my dad had an answer and it has stuck with me over the years. He stood up—at least this is the way he tells it—he stood up and made a speech. He said that the goal of a parent isn't merely to keep a child from physical harm. The goal of a parent is also to teach a child how to cope with the danger and excitement of the world. He liked the idea of a porch without a railing because then he would have to teach his children to take care. Obviously you wouldn't leave an infant or a toddler alone on a porch with a four-foot drop. But it would be wise, he said, to give an older child the responsibility of taking care not to fall off the porch. A four-foot drop was an excellent height to learn such a lesson. If you messed up, you might be merely bruised, you might break a leg, you—"

"You might break a neck," Laura interjected.

"That's right, and that made the alderman feel self-righteous about treating my dad like some kind of lunatic. But my dad understood that breaking your neck was incredibly unlikely. And that if you put up railings everywhere, your life was poorer for it. Not just because you weren't able to give a child the responsibility to learn how to cope with danger, but also because seven-year-olds like to get close to the edge of a four-foot porch and sometimes they like to jump. My dad used to say 'danger and delight grow on the same stalk.'"

"That's a nice line."

"He said it was an English proverb. He also used to say that it's good to feel the grass between your toes. Even if there might be a snake in the backyard, the wise man goes barefoot."

"Nor can foot feel, being shod," Laura said, almost to herself, her mind elsewhere for the moment.

"Excuse me?" Sam asked. "Shod? As in shoddy?"

"No. It just means wearing shoes. 'Nor can foot feel, being shod.' It's from a poem by Gerard Manley Hopkins. Nineteenth century. He was trying to say that our pursuit of material comfort erodes our ability to truly feel."

"My father didn't teach us a lot of poetry, but I think he'd like the line."

"So your dad lost."

"Yeah. I imagine he came home burning mad."

"Kind of the way you came home from that dinner party with that doctor, I would guess."

"A week later, we had a railing."

"How did your mom feel?"

"She kept quiet about it. But years later, she told me she had been glad that my dad had failed that night. She and my dad didn't always see eye-to-eye on danger and delight."

"I guess we don't either," Laura said.

"Fair enough. And vive la différence."

Laura smiled. She wondered how long the list of differences might be.

"The point is," Sam continued, "it's bad enough for the government to keep children away from dangerous porches. It's worse to treat adults like children, putting fences up everywhere to create a world of little danger. Not only is there less delight in a world of little danger, but there is less humanity when we are always being treated like children."

"Why? Do you think it makes us meaner?"

"No. That's not what I mean by less humanity. I mean less of what makes us essentially human."

"But why does a safer world make us less human?"

"Part of the essence of being human is making choices. It's anticipating the future and being aware of the costs and benefits of our actions. If you take the risk out of the future, you take away the choice and the challenge of grappling with the risk and

reward. You take away the responsibility. Children don't antici-
pate the future very well, so we treat children differently from
adults. But when we start treating adults like children, we start
taking away the essential human challenge of coping with uncertainty and making decisions."

"But helmet laws are different."

"Why?"

"Because if some jerk without insurance splats himself on
the highway I'm going to end up paying for his hospital bills. It
seems to me I have the right to keep his head in one piece."

"That's why it's like the V-8 juice. Of course you have the right.
A father doling out the allowance has the right to be paternalistic.
I wonder what the politically correct phrase would be." Sam peered
at the ceiling of the subway car as if the answer were written there.
"Parentalistic? Ugly-sounding word, don't you think?"

"Oh, I don't know," Laura countered. "It might grow on you
in time."

"Sounds like a fungus to me. Anyway, it does seem charitable
to guarantee medical assistance to people without insurance or
without the ability to pay. After that magnanimous gesture, why
spoil it by treating the pauper as a child and putting conditions on
how he or she is to live life? If you're going to be charitable, be
charitable. Why not say, 'I accept you for who you are and I am
willing to help you on your terms'? Of course, I don't believe that
there should be laws guaranteeing medical assistance to people
who splat themselves on the highway—"

"You're kidding, right? It's one thing to let people wander off
a porch. But how can you be against helping people who can't
afford to help themselves? It's just selfish, it's evil—"

"Evil?" Sam asked with wonder. "Evil?"

"OK, maybe just satanic. Until now, I had you to the right of Genghis Khan but to the left of Attila the Hun. You are rapidly moving Hun-ward."

"Welcome to the wonderful world of economics. Everything precious in life has a cost."

Laura looked at him and laughed.

"You were right," she said. "You're not easily offended."

"If you had my views, you'd get used to being insulted."

"If I had your views, Sam, I'd read more on the Metro and talk less."

"And if you had my views, you would be lonely and embattled, but you could take solace in being right."

Sam smiled at her sweetly. Laura couldn't decide whether the smile was an attempt to indicate a joke or whether he was trying to soften the brazenness of his claim. She tended to rely on Freud's dictum that there are no jokes.

"I can't figure you out," she said. "Your self-confidence borders on arrogance, but you aren't comfortable imposing your views on others. You're against helping people without health care, but you give money to beggars. And what about that poster in your classroom of Jimmy Stewart and Donna Reed. What's that doing there?"

"That's exactly where it belongs. See you around."

It was Sam's stop. Before Laura could ask him to explain, he was gone.

Four TÊTE À TÊTE

Charles Krauss, the CEO of HealthNet, sits impassively behind his desk. Across the expanse of black marble, he skeptically eyes the man sitting on the other side. Howard Cantrell shifts his weight in the chair from one haunch to the other. He methodically buttons and unbuttons the blue blazer he is wearing, unsure of the proper etiquette. The jacket shifts. A gap opens up behind his neck between the jacket and his shirt collar. The lapels bulge awkwardly.

"Yes?" Krauss asks finally, tired of waiting for the man to speak.

"We've got a problem."

Krauss gets up from his chair. Unconsciously he buttons the coat of his hand-tailored $2000 suit from Hong Kong and smoothes the lapels. He walks over to the wall on his right, a wall of mostly glass, that looks onto a courtyard. A gardener, stooped and old, makes swirling patterns with his rake in the fine white stone of a Japanese garden. Krauss watches the man for a moment. He does not have to turn his head back to his desk to know that the man sitting there still fidgets nervously, undulating like an eel.

"Tell me, Cantrell, how long have you been Director of Research?" Krauss refuses to look at the man. Instead, he continues to watch the gardener. The visitor starts to rise from the chair in order to respond to the question. He's not happy to be discussing his employment history over the distance that now lies between him and his boss, a distance of perhaps ten yards from his seat to where Krauss stands gazing out the window. But he is also uncomfortable coming around the desk. Too aggressive, he worries. He lowers himself back into the chair.

"Four years," he says.

Krauss wheels away from the window and stands over the desk. "I'm sure your lab is busy."

Cantrell nods.

"Maybe you're spending too much time in the lab," Krauss continues, "and not enough time managing your people." Krauss leans forward on the desk and though the desk is large, he appears to loom over the other man like a shadow. "Director of Research is a position of responsibility. Your job is to solve problems. My job is to run this company."

"I know. I intend to solve the problem. I—I *will* solve the problem," he says, correcting himself. "But I thought you should know what's going on. The clinical trials for the new prostate drug are not going well. I'm worried. It affects the entire corporation. We've got too much riding on this product. We've got to start preparing for a potential downside. I think—"

"I really don't care what you think. I don't pay you to think. I especially don't pay you to think about corporate strategy. I pay you to run the research department and run it well. Fix the problem. We've been there before. You know what to do. I'm sure you can handle it."

There is nothing on Krauss's desk other than a laptop computer off to one side. Its black matte cover is a faint shadow against the burnished black marble of the desk. Krauss pulls the computer to the center of the desk, flips it open and brings it to life. In an instant, his mind is poring over the numbers on the screen, looking for opportunity. The interview is over.

"Absolutely. No problem," Cantrell says, rising out of the chair and edging toward the door. He pauses. His body is at rest for the first time since entering the office. "I just wanted you to know. In case something goes wrong. I know how you hate surprises."

"Your job is to make sure that nothing goes wrong. There is one thing I hate more than surprises. Failure. You know our numbers last quarter were unacceptable. If Prostol doesn't live up to its advanced billing, our stock will take another dip down the roller coaster. I don't need to explain that to the business press. Don't screw up."

Cantrell smiles in an attempt to show that he has no intention of screwing up. He edges back out of the office. Krauss's head is down, lost in the spreadsheet. He looks up for a moment and sees that the man is gone. Krauss closes his eyes, takes a deep breath and shakes his head.

∞

There is no conference room, so the Monday morning staff meeting at the Office of Corporate Responsibility takes place in a corner of the office of the director, Erica Baldwin. The chairs arranged in a loose circle in the open space beyond her desk are a hodgepodge. Some are standard government-issue gray metal. One is an upholstered monstrosity in synthetic orange, another, lollipop green.

This Monday morning, five women and three men make their way into the office. Erica Baldwin is probably the oldest, and she is only thirty-six. The staffers wear business casual. Only Erica Baldwin is dressed formally in a fitted navy blue suit in case she has to go up to the Hill.

The meeting begins with a review of last week's calls to the Corporate Responsibility Hot Line, 1-800-CORP-RES, established by the OCR to ferret out corporate misbehavior. Today, there is the usual smorgasbord of complaints. One caller works on the assembly line for an auto manufacturer. A car model has shown serious instability on turns and the company has destroyed the test results.

"There are no federal standards for stability like there are for mileage and bumper safety," Erica Baldwin explains to the younger staffers, shaking her head. Another caller, a woman, complains of sexual harassment at the oil company where she works.

Erica Baldwin asks for volunteers to follow up on these leads and the others presented. Most will be dead ends. Some will be referred to other government agencies, OSHA, the FDA, the FTC, or the EEOC, who have the official jurisdiction over the relevant issue. But others will become part of ongoing or new investigations of the OCR into cases of corporate irresponsibility, behavior that is reprehensible but for now, beyond the reach of the law.

Erica then asks Marshall Jackson to give the group an update on the HealthNet investigation. Jackson, one of two African-Americans on the staff, straightens up in his chair. He has an MBA from Wharton. He graduated first in his class at Harvard Law. These two degrees and his raw intelligence are a formidable combination. He has been at the OCR for less than a year, but already he is in charge of the investigation of HealthNet.

"Talking about HealthNet is like talking about a career criminal," he begins. "You get your full range of activity from misdemeanors up to homicide. Here in the states, they've laid off thousands, shifting production overseas. None of their senior executives is a woman or African-American. There are serious concerns about their pharmaceutical products' safety. Overseas they exploit their workers using underpaid kids to assemble the medical devices they sell all over the world. Their drug pricing is unconscionable."

Jackson proceeds to lay out the details in each of the areas along with some of the supporting evidence and data. When he is finished, Erica Baldwin asks the group for their opinion on how best to proceed with the investigation. Some staffers argue for congressional hearings into the company's practices. They'd be preliminary to a formal citation of irresponsibility by the OCR and potentially, investigations by other government agencies. But others on the staff urge caution. The question is one of timing.

Erica Baldwin listens carefully to the different arguments. She says little, content to let her staff explore the pros and cons of the various possibilities. Finally, when the discussion winds down, she speaks to the issue.

"In my opinion, we're not ready," she says. The staff reacts with surprise. Baldwin is known for her aggressiveness. "We're missing a piece of the puzzle," she continues. "I'm not sure what that piece is. Right now, what we have is fairly standard stuff. The range of misdeeds is impressive, but I want something that will put HealthNet over the top even in the minds of the average American. And when we find that bit of corporate misbehavior, we'll know it. It will make the case decisive. What do you think?"

Decisions at the OCR are made by consensus. The staff often defers to the director's judgment, but not always. Today, they agree with Erica Baldwin's assessment. They agree to wait. The meeting is over. There is a flurry of chit-chat and friendly banter as the room empties. Baldwin asks Marshall Jackson to stay behind.

"You didn't have much to say, Marshall, once you finished your report. Are you getting shy on me?"

Marshall laughs. He is a gentle giant towering over the shorter woman. Erica sometimes worries whether he is too cerebral for the OCR. He needs seasoning in the ways of Washington.

"I trust your instincts," he answers. "What I don't understand is what you hope to gain by waiting. Don't we have plenty of dirt on them already?"

"We do," Baldwin replies. "But it's just dirt. I want mud. We hold hearings now and what happens? A slap on the wrist for HealthNet. They'll get some bad publicity, maybe an investigation by the FDA or the EEOC."

Marshall Jackson says nothing. Erica Baldwin goes over to the one window in her office. She looks out and sees the building's rusty dumpsters.

"The OCR wouldn't even be here if there hadn't been that second oil spill off the Alaska coast," she says, almost to herself. "But we're nothing. Wedged into a corner of the FTC's building with makeshift offices. Barely enough staff to get the job done. Congress throws us a bone now and then, but we're mainly mucking about in the garbage looking for something the other agencies have missed."

"So remind me again why I took this job," Jackson says. "I thought I work here to make a difference."

"We do, we do," Baldwin answers, pacing in front of him, her hands gesturing in excitement. "I took this job for the upside potential. If we nail HealthNet and their CEO, we can be something more than a watchdog agency. We can be the nerve center for the FDA, the FTC, OSHA, and the EEOC. Instead of fiddling around the edges of the problems they've rejected, we can put the whole picture together. We could even get a shot at

Cabinet status. We could finally get the teeth we need to shake up the corporate world."

Erica Baldwin moves away from the window and stands in front of Marshall Jackson. The stridency in her voice is gone now.

"You're an important player on this team, Marshall," she says. "Your background in regulatory law will be a key part of the HealthNet investigation. You know that, don't you?"

"I do."

"I wish I could pay you even half of what you turned down at that New York law firm. I hope the thrill of the chase makes up for it. And let me tell you. It's going to be some chase. Charles Krauss will do everything in his considerable power to keep us from doing our job. Be prepared to play hardball. It's the only game Krauss knows. But I promise, in the end, we'll make a difference."

Marshall Jackson nods and heads to his office. He is too inexperienced to know much about the thrill of the chase. But he's glad to be on the same side as Erica Baldwin. He has never met Charles Krauss. But he doubts that even Krauss can withstand the efforts of Erica Baldwin to bring him down.

Five UNDERPAID AND OVERWORKED

Laura Silver sat at her desk in her empty classroom on a December afternoon, preparing her lesson plans for the next day. It had already been a long day of teaching, and now she was having trouble concentrating on the task at hand. Maybe a cup of coffee would help. She headed to the teacher's lounge.

The halls were empty. Entering the lounge, she was surprised to see Sam Gordon sitting on one of the couches, sipping a cup of tea, reading. It had been two weeks since their ride home on the subway. That discussion had ended unpleasantly. Still, she found it a relief to see him here in the lounge. He was a welcome distraction.

"What are you doing here?" she asked.

"I work here, remember?"

"Funny. Everybody else seems to have gone home."

"I'm just tying up some loose ends. How about you?"

"I'm trying to find the loose ends. I'm trying to keep from going under." Laura emptied the dead pot of coffee into the sink and started a fresh one. Then she took a seat on the couch. "Tell me it gets easier."

"Sure it does. What are you working on?"

"Have you read *Great Expectations*?"

"Who's it by?" Sam asked sheepishly.

"An old English guy, name of Dickens. Have you heard of *him*?

"Yes, I've heard of him," Sam said in exasperation. "He wrote *A Tale of Two Cities*. Read it in high school. But I'm afraid we didn't get to *Great Expectations*."

"It might have changed your life. Saved you from a career in economics," Laura said, laughing. "Actually I think you'd like it. It's a story of money earned and unearned. A story of high and low, poor and mighty. It's a pretty good page-turner. And the original movie version's not bad either. I need a homework assignment for tomorrow," she said, coming down from her enthusiasm in telling Sam about the book. "We're just about finished with it, so I need a final assignment to wrap things up. You did say it gets easier, right?"

"Sure. It took me two years before I had my classes even remotely under control. I was like you. Up late every night working on the next day's classes. Or grading some assignment. Teaching, despite a widespread belief to the contrary, takes a lot of energy. Especially if you want to do it right. If you're lazy, you can get away with the same assignments every year. The students won't know. But *you* will and it makes you stale. So if you want to do it right, you should always plan on working hard."

"Great. So we're not just underpaid, we're overworked."

"We're not underpaid," Sam said, cocking his head to one side and looking at her quizzically. How could she think they were underpaid?

"We're not underpaid? Maybe you're raking it in because you teach economics. I'm making $26,000 in our nation's capital. I'm underpaid."

"I don't know what underpaid means—"

"Don't be a sophist," Laura interrupted.

"What's a sophist?"

"Someone who manipulates words and ideas for the delight of manipulation rather than for the sake of truth. For your future reference, it's a mildly pejorative term."

"No problem. I really don't know what underpaid means. When people say they are underpaid, they usually mean they wish they earned more. In which case, everyone is underpaid. Or thinks they are. In fact most people do think that way. I find it striking how many people resent their economic condition when it's so much more pleasant to be content with what you have."

"You should expect resentment when teachers earn $26,000 and CEOs, athletes, and movie stars earn millions."

"What's wrong with that?"

Laura got up from the couch. Her long skirt ebbed and flowed as she paced in front of him. Sam watched as she stopped and pulled her hair back and secured it with a large barrette. She did it fiercely, her mind working to sort out her thoughts. Then she faced him.

"Fair?" she finally blurted out. "How can you compare the instruction of the next generation to bouncing a leather ball on a hardwood floor?"

"Let me try. We educate between 30 and 150 kids per year. A great athlete will entertain millions."

"But one exercise is frivolous and the other is sublime."

"I quite agree. Which is why I teach high school rather than—"

"Play basketball?" Laura said mockingly.

"No," Sam continued, unperturbed. "It's why I teach high school rather than do something else with my economics degree that pays more."

"I commend your self-sacrifice. But you haven't answered my point. One is frivolous and the other sublime."

"Which is which?" Sam asked.

"Very funny. You just admitted that you prefer teaching high school to making more money."

"That's the way *I* feel. But the artistry of a basketball player is only frivolous in your eyes. To others, he's a genius. Would you admit that he should make at least as much money as a psychiatrist? They both help people forget their troubles."

Sam put his hands behind his head, leaned back and grinned. "The real point," Sam continued, "is that the world is a wondrous place and our talents are diverse. Even more wondrous is that in America you are free to be whatever you would be. I wasn't born to be an economist or a basketball player or a plumber. I could have chosen a completely different mix of prestige and money and excitement. But I chose to be an economics teacher. That's the choice that's best for me. But I doubt it's best for you."

"Amen," Laura said, pouring herself a cup of coffee and sitting down on the opposite end of the couch from Sam. She pulled her legs up under her skirt. "You sound like Dr. Pangloss."

"Who?"

"Dr. Pangloss, in Voltaire's *Candide*. He always said that we live in the best of all possible worlds because we make our own choices using free will. But Voltaire was satirizing the appeal of free will. Sometimes the best choice that's available is still ghastly. Just because you or I freely chose to become teachers doesn't change the fact that teaching pays poorly."

"It depends on your yardstick. A teacher in America today has a standard of living that surpasses the standard of living of most of humanity through most of human history. You just think it has more intrinsic merit than other professions. But merit is in the eye of the beholder. Under the market system, there is no beholder. No one explicitly makes the decision about how many jobs of one type or other there should be, or the pay structure. The decision gets made by the impersonal forces of the marketplace."

"That sounds more like an indictment than high praise. It means no one's in charge, doesn't it? It means that everyone is out for themselves. It means no one is watching over the system to make sure it's fair."

"You're right. That's a virtue, not a flaw. It's a system where the power is spread out rather than concentrated in the hands of a limited number of people. It's like the rain forest. If you leave it alone, it does fine by itself. No one is in charge except the rules that govern the overall system. In economic systems, having no one in charge disperses power. That dispersion of power prevents corruption unless everyone is corrupt. And if everyone is corrupt, you have a society that no system can tame. But in a system where power is concentrated at the top, the temptation for corruption at the top is almost unavoidable. I love that no one's in control."

"I don't see how you can praise a system that makes CEOs and basketball players the lords of the manor and makes us the serfs."

Now Sam sprang up from the couch and paced. He and Laura were so engrossed in their conversation that neither noticed the janitor come in to empty the trash. It was past five o'clock.

"What's the alternative?" Sam asked, stretching out his long arms in supplication. "If we arbitrarily raise the salaries of high school teachers, then more people will want to be teachers than there are jobs available. How are you going to decide who gets the $100,000 per year or $1 million per year high-school teaching jobs? A lottery? Will that produce dedicated teachers? Or maybe you should appoint a benevolent teaching czar who would pick the best teachers for the high-paying teaching jobs. But how long could the czar stay benevolent? When the salary is say, $100,000, the would-be teachers will quickly realize that there are not

enough jobs to go around. They won't wait for the announce-
ments. They'll begin to lean on the czar in subtle and not so subtle ways to influence the decision. Who will keep the system
benevolent in such a world?"

"There are decent people in the world. Corruption isn't
inevitable. A board or committee could make sure that the best
teachers get chosen."

"I don't know. In the wrong system, there are no decent people. Or they get pushed aside by the not so decent ones. We can't
imagine what it's like to live in a world where the power to make
economic decisions is centralized," Sam answered. "My sister
lives in Houston. When a lot of Russian Jews came to the United
States in the late 1980s, she and her husband became a host family—they volunteered to help the new immigrants get used to the
United States, take them around until they bought a car and so on.
On one of their first nights in the United States, my sister took this
Russian couple to the grocery. It was a normal American grocery.
You walk in, grab a cart and the first thing you see is the produce
section. The Russians went crazy. They wanted to cry with joy.
They'd never seen such a cornucopia. They filled their cart with
grapes and oranges and pears and melons—fruits that in the former Soviet Union were only available to Communist Party members or on the black market at prices they could never afford.
Eventually, my sister got them to explore the rest of the store. The
Russian woman wanted some yeast. They couldn't find any. My
sister was embarrassed. Here, in the land of plenty, no yeast? So
she found the store manager—he went into the back and brought
out a box with two dozen packets of yeast. The Russian woman took
a couple and the manager wandered off to put the rest out on the

shelves. No big deal, right? But the Russian woman is beaming at my sister. Do you know why? Because she assumed that my sister must be some big shot if she can get the manager to bring out the special stuff kept in the back for the special customers, just like in the Soviet Union. We can't imagine what it's like to live in a system where the yeast or the meat or the fruit or the good jobs or the apartments are handed out depending on whether you're a member of the right party or you know the right people. It's horrifying."

"But our system is like that too. To get a job you have to impress the boss."

"That's true. But there are thousands of bosses, and the boss that hires sycophants or people who offer bribes ends up with an organization that performs poorly."

"I still come back to my earlier point. If our system works so well, why can't it pay a teacher a living wage?"

"Are you dying? There's a healthy waiting list of people who want to teach here. If you want to blame someone, blame us, the teachers. There are too many people willing to teach at the going rate. That keeps the wages low. And if you'd like some solace, think about why—it's a great job. You get summers off and once you get the hang of it, you can go home at 3:30 most days. If you're any good at it, you also get the ecstasy of watching the light bulb come on in a young mind. That joy is a key part of the pay package. Savor it. And be grateful you're not in a job that's so repugnant it pays a salary premium to attract workers."

"I like that," Laura admitted. "But most teachers take low wages because they don't have better alternatives."

"I disagree. They're free to pursue whatever they like—many of them have much better paying alternatives."

"But those who don't are stuck. I'm sorry. It seems cruel."

"Cruel? 'Cruel' is torturing a cat or taking candy from a child. But I agree that economic life has its ups and downs. If you know a way to remove the tough times and keep the life, let me know."

"Can't you remove a *little bit* of the hardship and keep *most* of the life?"

"Touché." Sam paused. His mind wandered for a moment. "Do you think *I'm* cruel?" he asked with what seemed to be genuine interest.

"I'm trying to keep an open mind," Laura replied. "You've moved up from satanic at any rate. But I still think I'm underpaid."

"Then leave. Go get an MBA. Deal drugs. Work harder. Take a second job on the side. Don't complain. Do something about it. It's easy to blame the system, but it's in your hands. Unless you want to have your cake and eat it too. *That* the system does not allow. Sometimes the best jobs, the ones that are sublime, pay less because so many people are competing to get at them."

"Then why do athletes make so much? Doesn't everyone want a life of fame and glory?"

"Many do. But not everyone can mix basketball and ballet like a Michael Jordan. When the supply is small, the wage is high. So even though being a professional athlete appeals to millions, the wages stay high."

"Then how do you explain the CEOs who make millions? Where's the artistry in slashing jobs and cutting wages? Why does every CEO, good or bad, make so much money?"

"When my students first come into my course, they think being a CEO means sitting at a big desk counting your money, drinking coffee and talking on the phone from time to time. They think it's a job that gets handed out through some lottery. The losers flip hamburgers for minimum wage."

"You mean it doesn't work that way?"

"Very funny. Maybe you ought to sit in on my class," Sam said whimsically. "You'd find that CEOs work harder than you imagine. Running an enormous enterprise is harder than it looks. I suspect that mediocre CEOs make a lot of money for the same reason that a bench player in the NBA can still make millions. He looks mediocre but he does a much better job than you or I could do. But the system is imperfect. Some CEOs make a lot of money because the board of directors is weak. Some CEOs mislead their boards of directors by manipulating financial information to suit their self-interests. And plenty of CEOs make mistakes, honestly or not, that harm their employees, their customers or their stockholders. But irresponsible or incompetent CEOs find it harder to find work. The system punishes despots. Mean vicious CEOs find it harder and harder to get people to work for them. They find it harder and harder to get people to hire them. That's what makes the system self-regulating. The beauty of the system is that the power to hire and fire is in the hands of the person who is accountable for seeing the enterprise survive. It's an extraordinarily effective method. I prefer that solution to giving economic power to a committee or a board or a government agency in Washington. That creates another kind of despot, one who's even further removed from accountability."

"I'm more trusting of bureaucrats, Sam. Some of them are family. So maybe I'm biased."

"I understand. But I'm serious about cutting back on resentment," he continued. "Life is much better when you don't resent your circumstances. So if you hate making $26,000, stop moping and do something about it."

"I suppose it's too early in my teaching career to know whether I'll end up liking it or not. But I *am* planning to go to law school."

Laura paused, partly for dramatic effect, partly to catch her breath. She thought he would applaud her plan. She was unprepared for his response.

"Bad idea," Sam said, without thinking.

"Why?" Laura found her voice rising defensively.

"Never mind. It would take a long time, I'd have ruined your life by the time we were done, and you might hate me for it. Besides, I'm starving. Want to get something to eat?"

"With the man who could ruin my life?" Laura arched an eyebrow and hoped she was keeping some dignity in the face of his arrogance. "I've got to get back to work."

Sam shrugged and watched Laura retreat to the privacy of her classroom. Not a very gracious close to the conversation, he thought. He'd have to do better next time.

Sam went over to the mail slots to check his mail. There was the usual collection of junk mail from textbook publishers. There was also an envelope with his name and CONFIDENTIAL stamped in red on it. He sat down to read.

Dear Mr. Gordon:

We spoke last week concerning certain allegations about your conduct that had come to my attention. I have now conducted several interviews with students. I regret to inform you that their testimony essentially bears out the allegations we discussed.

Based on my investigation and discussions I have had with key members of the board, I am forced to recommend dismissal. School policy requires a vote of the entire board to affirm my decision. Should they do so, you will have an opportunity to appeal.

This decision and all of the details will remain confidential. It does not serve the Edwards School or yourself to make them public. No charges will be brought; if you feel it is in your best interest to look for other employment and avoid a formal decision by the board, we will accommodate you.

Sincerely,

Franklin Harkin

Principal

Six TURNING OUT THE LIGHTS

"As many of you already know, I have some bad news."

The man speaking, George Sutherland, stands on a chair in the corner of a vast warehouse attached to a factory. He looks out at the sea of anxious faces. Some are in suits and ties, but most of the 300 or so people are wearing work clothes.

"I was born in this town. I started right here in this ware-house, as a stocker. I've worked here, either part-time or full-time, for most of my adult life. I had expected to retire here. Many of you had the same plans. But as you probably have heard, the corporation that owns this plant, HealthNet, has decided to close it and send everything to Mexico. Sometime next month, all of the inventory in this warehouse will be shipped out. The production facility next door will also be shut down."

Sutherland looks down at the floor for the moment. He is trying to regain his composure. He does not like looking at the bitterness in the faces of so many good people. As he looks down, he notices that the floor is spotless. The whole place is like that. Everything is as tidy as his garage back home. Every-thing is in its place. Pride surges up in him when he thinks of these people and the job they do.

"You are the backbone of this company. It has been an honor and a joy to manage this facility. By law, HealthNet is required to give you three months notice. In addition, there will be an extra payment of $50 at the end of this month."

He almost chokes on the words. The crowd greets the announcement with curses and shouts. George Sutherland waits for them vent their anger and for the room to go quiet again.

"I don't blame you for being angry. I'm angry too. I know it's not fair and it's not right. But for now, that's the way it is. If I can help you in any way, my door is open. I'll see you tomorrow."

The people file out of the building. George Sutherland stays behind. He loves the feel of a deserted warehouse, the sound of his shoes squeaking on the clean floor and echoing upward. He first started working here as a part-time job in high school, working in the office, and then driving a forklift. He used to love the expanse of this building, its high ceilings and endless rows of neatly stacked material. When he was here he could forget about how small his house was. He felt free here.

He tries to look into the future, but he can't imagine a world without this plant, without this job. He sees the forklifts, lined up for the night in the slots where they belong. There used to be a squadron of them, maybe eight or ten. Now there are only two. Nostalgia sweeps over him and he takes a seat in one, starts it up and follows one of the old stocking routes he used to know so well. Following the swath of blue paint along the floor that marks the route, he sees in his mind's eye the younger man he once was, following the same route late on the night of his twentieth birthday. He had bet one of the other forklift drivers that he could drive the Blue route with his eyes closed. And he did it, but the guy refused to pay. Said he must have cheated. George didn't care. He loved the mastery of the thing and that was all that mattered.

A few of his high-school buddies had gone on to Ohio State. But not George. Who needed a college education back then? A factory job waited for anyone willing to work hard. But now the factories were closing all over America. Where would his kids end up?

Driving the forklift tonight clears his head. The throaty surge of the engine wipes away all the words he had spoken earlier. They were no good. No words could have been. He puts the forklift back where it belongs, then steps outside and locks up. The parking lot has emptied out. There is no night shift any more. That work has already been sent elsewhere.

Better to leave the car in the lot and walk home. He needs time to think, time to figure out what to say to his wife and family who are waiting for him. He knows it won't be easy, but he also knows that all over town, men and women will tell their families that the other shoe finally fell, the work is gone. Most will not be financially or emotionally prepared to deal with the challenge.

The town will take a beating, too. It's like any other small town in Ohio or anywhere else. A lot of families with the same hopes and dreams. And tonight, sitting around the supper table, fathers and mothers will have to tell their children that hard times are coming. The vacation will be postponed. The bike won't get bought now. The braces will have to wait. The new car is out of the question. The second car will have to be sold.

Wives and older children who are at home will have to look for work. But it's a small town. There won't be enough work to go around. Not by a long shot. Plenty of businesses will go broke because too many customers will be without paychecks. It will be a time to tighten the belt and pray for help to come. It is going to be tough for a long, long time.

George Sutherland is not a pessimistic man. But as he thinks about what is going to happen to his town and to his family, he stops at the bench under the big oak in the center of town and sits for a while with his head buried in his hands. Finally, he rises and heads north on Maple Street. The road climbs slightly.

Three blocks up ahead, he can see the light burning on the porch. Making an effort, he puts a swing into his stride and a smile on his face for his waiting wife and kids.

∞

Charles Krauss drives a golf ball the same way he drives a car, the same way he drives his employees, the same way he does everything, with absolute confidence and a touch of ferocity. He rips into the ball with the oversized driver and the ball rockets into the perfect blue sky and bounds down the narrow-wooded fairway, coming to rest almost 250 yards away.

"Nice shot, sir."

Krauss says nothing. He is thinking about his next shot. The man who has paid the compliment, Rob Blankenship, Health-Net's Director of Corporate Communication, waggles his club readying his tee shot. In deference to the difficulty of the opening hole, he chooses a 3-wood rather than risk the driver.

The first swing of the day is always challenging. Playing with Charles Krauss adds to the pressure. Inevitably, the match becomes competitive. And does Blankenship really want to beat his boss? In fact, it's not really an option. Though he is the younger man, he usually loses by anywhere from three to five strokes even when he's trying to do his best.

To Blankenship's great relief, his swing and follow through feel good. "Stay left, stay left," Blankenship urges quietly as he lifts his head to watch the ball. On a normal course, Blankenship's drive would be respectable. But this course is unforgiving. Krauss had it built two years ago, adjacent to the company's headquarters. On this first hole, the Virginia pine forest hugs the right side of the fairway, eagerly awaiting an errant shot.

The ball hits the fairway once, then dives into the woods. Blankenship curses under his breath.

"You lifted your elbow," Krauss says accusingly.

Blankenship gives a quick nod of acknowledgment and tries to calm his anger and frustration. Asking for a mulligan is out of the question.

The two men get into the cart. Blankenship is at the wheel. He would prefer to be sitting in Krauss's office, unpleasant as that can be, than to be out here, pretending he is having a good time and trying to get some work accomplished in these spare moments in the cart. But this is the way Krauss likes it. He was thrilled to discover that Blankenship played golf. Krauss hates PR issues and finds them palatable only when taken with the sweetener of a golf game.

Blankenship leaps from the cart when they reach the spot where his ball made like a rabbit and skipped into the woods. He gives up quickly after a perfunctory search. Krauss gets annoyed if his partner spends too long trying to find a lost ball. After all, Krauss is in a position for a birdie and his hunger to hit his second shot and get onto the green is palpable. Blankenship drops a new ball near where his was lost. He plays it safe and lays up well short of the green.

Krauss shakes his head disapprovingly at his partner's lack of nerve. He takes out a seven iron, and—thwack!—lofts a perfect parabola onto the green, fifteen feet from the hole. Then he waits impatiently for Blankenship to get onto the green and two-putt for a seven. Finally, Krauss putts for the birdie. The ball curls around the cup and drops. Krauss grunts in satisfaction.

Blankenship manages to par the second hole, a short par three, but by the end of four holes, Krauss holds a five-stroke lead. Krauss will win, but there will be the semblance of competition, which is the way Krauss likes it. So all in all, the day is not going badly. This emboldens Blankenship to talk business.

"Have you given any thought to that Ohio factory, the one in Matalon?" he asks, as they head to the fifth tee.

"Of course I have." Krauss eyes Blankenship's profile as if his chauffeur were a madman. Blankenship keeps his eyes on the cart path. "It's a no-brainer," Krauss continues. "The plant in Matalon is unionized. By moving to Mexico we can add $20 million to the bottom line over the next five years. That's $20 million after-tax."

"I know. I wrote the press release. I meant have you given any thought to the bigger picture."

"What bigger picture?"

"The town is going to be hit pretty hard. We're the biggest employer there. There's going to be a lot of negative coverage."

Again, Krauss looks over at Blankenship.

"Your job is to prevent that kind of coverage. What are you doing about it?"

"I haven't had much luck so far. I've tried to sell some stories about how some of our American plants will be increasing their exports to supply the Mexican plant, but I haven't been able to get much play."

"Try harder."

"I will. I was just wondering if it might be a good idea to make a donation to the local United Way, a small donation really, a goodwill gesture, you know, boost the local economy, help some of the charities in the town, and then,—"

"And what do you consider a 'small donation'?"

"I don't know, maybe $100,000. That's less than a decent retraining program would cost, and it's only about one dollar for each resident there. It would be a way for us to show that we care, that we—"

"We've already spent almost $100,000 in severance pay. Totally unnecessary. That's what you ought to be getting the press to talk about. We've done our part. Whose side are you on, Blankenship?"

Blankenship says nothing more about the plant in Matalon. He has given it his best shot. His thoughts turn to the next hole, a 590-yard par five.

∞

All the lights in Erica Baldwin's Georgetown townhouse are off save the one over the most comfortable seat in the house, a big overstuffed armchair. She sits there in her gray sweats, her feet tucked under her, going over documents as she does every night before going to bed. The mass of red hair carelessly piled on top of her head combines with her round reading glasses to make her look like some strange breed of owl. She looks up from the document she is working on and catching sight of the clock, jumps up and switches on the television to catch the opening of the eleven o'clock news.

"Tonight's lead story: more embarrassment for Virginia-based HealthNet. Workers in Matalon, Ohio report shabby treatment at the hands of the health conglomerate. We have a report from our Cleveland affiliate, WNSN."

"Thank you, Dan. We're here with Cathy Sutherland and her three children. Cathy's husband, George, has been the plant manager at HealthNet's facility here for almost ten years. How has this decision by HealthNet to relocate this plant affected your life?"

Erica watches the interview. The woman has an open and honest face that makes her words more effective. The children at her side also help. She tells the interviewer how she may not be able to make her mortgage payments. Behind her, a group of workers carry pickets complaining about HealthNet's decision to leave the town.

Erica had received a call telling her that the story would run. The story may force her hand. There will be increased pressure from Congress for hearings. She may have no choice but to instigate a formal OCR investigation into HealthNet. She is still waiting for the piece of the puzzle that will turn an OCR investigation into the juggernaut she knows it can be. Until she has it, she will try to bide her time.

∞

To the south, in an apartment complex in Northern Virginia, a young woman sits in bed, running a brush over and over again through her long blond hair. She is also watching the eleven o'clock news. She watches the mother with the three children tell of her concerns about her mortgage. The story ends and the anchorman comes back on.

"If your employer is acting irresponsibly and if you'd like to let someone know, call the hotline at the Office of Corporate Responsibility at 1-800-CORP-RES. That's 1-800-CORP-RES."

The woman drops the hairbrush and scrambles off the bed to copy down the number. She has come to a decision.

Seven EXPLOITING THE CONSUMER

"It comes to $20.40, Ms. Silver."

Laura wondered how dry cleaning four blouses could be so expensive. As she stood outside Capitol Cleaners on a January afternoon, reconsidering her devotion to silk and linen, Sam Gordon came hustling along, bringing his own shirts for cleaning. He stopped in surprise.

"Hey, Laura." He looked down at his watch. "Only 4:15 and you're out and about. Congratulations. Your lessons ready for tomorrow?"

"No, I'll be doing them tonight. I've got errands to run. I can't believe how expensive women's dry cleaning is," Laura said, almost to herself.

"Hold that thought, I'll be right back."

Despite Capitol Cleaners' proximity to the Edwards School, Laura was a little surprised to see Sam there. Heavily wrinkled cotton button-downs seemed to be the centerpiece of his wardrobe. She was pleased to see that he had mastered dry cleaning even if his visits were sporadic. Sam came back and found Laura sitting on a bench in the park next door.

"How many shirts did you just drop off?" she asked.

"Eight."

Laura fought off the urge to ask him how long eight shirts would hold him. Six months? A year?

"What do they charge you?" she asked instead.

"Only $1.50 each if I don't mind getting them back on Thursday."

"My four blouses cost more to clean than your eight shirts. Does that seem fair to you?"

"Economists are not very good at 'fair.' This has probably reduced our social image and popularity."

"One of many factors, no doubt. Just tell me if it's fair," Laura said.

"Let me ask you something first. Do you really want my opinion, or do you just want someone to reinforce your bitterness?"

Laura smiled.

"Another person's outrage can be very soothing," Sam continued. "I can't offer any outrage, but I think I can cheer you up."

"Go ahead." Laura prompted.

"As you might expect, I don't think fairness has anything to do with it. If you—"

"You only care about profits," Laura interrupted, her anger flaring again at Sam's apparent indifference, "and business's right to charge whatever the market will bear. That's your yardstick of fairness. It's a warped one if you ask me."

Laura sat back hard against the bench and crossed her arms.

"I see the soothing effect has yet to set in," Sam said. "Let's take a time-out. How about a cup of coffee?" Sam asked, gesturing up the block and across the street to The Mean Bean, the local coffee place.

"Oh, I guess," she said, hesitating.

"My treat."

"There I draw the line. I can still afford the occasional latte even with these dry-cleaning costs. I may have to look a bit more rumpled from now on."

"That's OK. I won't report you to the authorities."

"I guess I have time. Sure, let's go."

Laura wondered about Sam's relationship with the authorities at the Edwards School. She had heard talk that Sam was under some kind of investigation. Some even said that Sam would be gone after the school year was over. The source of these rumors was usually a student. She hadn't been teaching long enough to know if that made the rumors reliable.

The Mean Bean was mostly empty at this time of day. Just a few scattered customers sipping and reading. Sam and Laura made their way to the counter at the back. There was no one in line. Laura ordered a skim latte and Sam, a cup of tea. They took a table along the window at the front, Laura gently draping her new dry cleaning over an empty chair.

"Laura."

"Sam."

"Look. You've got me all wrong. By about 180 degrees. If you want to hear my take on it, fine. If you want to stew in resentment, we'll avoid dry cleaning and talk school politics instead. Your choice."

Laura was tempted to go for the school politics. She might discover the truth behind those rumors about Sam. She told herself it was pure nosiness rather than concern. Sam was surely too reactionary to ever become a close friend.

"Hey, I like stewing in resentment," she said, smiling.

"Most people do. I just think a world without stewing is a sweeter place."

"You're probably right. Go ahead."

"You think you're the victim of the dry cleaner. After all, the dry cleaner is greedy, isn't he?"

"I'll take that as a rhetorical question."

"But what's the best way to keep that greed from hurting the consumer?" Sam asked.

"You could start with a law that requires him to charge the same price for women's and men's shirts."

"That's one way, and a very costly one."

"Costly to whom? The dry cleaner?"

"Probably not, actually. Businesses are very creative at avoiding the costs of regulation. It's often the customer who ends up paying, one way or another. In this case, the dry cleaner will either raise the price of men's shirts or stop cleaning women's shirts in order to avoid being subject to the law. In your eagerness for justice, you'll punish the consumer. It would be better to find a solution that would protect the consumer and let those lawyers who would have argued the case do something more productive. That's why I favor doing nothing."

"Very appealing," Laura said sarcastically.

"Consider the greedy dry cleaner," Sam said, cheerfully ignoring Laura's reaction. "The higher the price he charges, the more money he makes. If he can lower his costs by making a shoddier product, he also increases his profits. So it's tempting to charge high prices for a crummy product."

"I've noticed. And you honor his right to do so." Laura found herself getting angrier than she was before. Sam could be so infuriating.

"I do. Now here's the question. Why would I feel the way I do? After all, I'm a customer. Why wouldn't I be worried about the dry cleaner's greed?"

Laura hesitated.

"I've never thought about it really," she said. "You think businesses have rights. I don't."

"But why would I believe in an idea that allows consumers to be exploited? Do I look like a pawn of business?"

Sam opened his arms wide for inspection. Laura laughed in spite of herself.

"Then why are you so tolerant of profits?"

"Because profits help the customer. The potential for profit spurs a business to please its customers. And when a business has competitors, gouging the customer just sends him out the door in search of alternatives. It's the same with wages and working conditions. You'd think every employer would like to offer his or her employees a $1000 a year and make them work 100 hours a week."

"Wouldn't they? Isn't that why we need unions and minimum-wage laws?"

"About 10 percent of the private sector workforce is unionized and less than 5 percent earns the minimum wage. So why do you think the other 85 percent or so makes tens of thousands of dollars above the minimum wage? How do we manage to avoid being exploited?"

"I've never thought about it. It's a good question."

"Since the mid-'50s, union membership as a percentage of the workforce has declined almost every year. Over that time, wages have grown, the work week has gotten shorter and all kinds of innovations have occurred—flextime, telecommuting, on-site day care, gyms in the workplace, you name it. And why would profit-hungry businesses offer these improvements? Competition. If you want to attract skilled workers, you have to offer them competitive wages and working conditions. You think you're underpaid at $26,000. Why doesn't the Edwards School pay even less? Because they can't if they want to attract quality teachers. It's the same with prices. If you want to attract customers, you have to keep prices just barely over your costs. Otherwise, one of your competitors can take your customers with lower prices or higher quality."

"Well maybe this competition theory is a little overrated. I read an exposé in the paper once about the dry cleaners. They get together and agree to keep prices high. Isn't that what really happens?"

"I doubt it. First of all, conspiring to fix prices is against the law. Second of all, if I were a dry cleaner and had figured out a way to collude with my fellow business owners to exploit customers, I'd pick men to exploit, not women. I bet there are a lot more men's shirts getting dry-cleaned than women's blouses. But let's suppose it *is* a conspiracy to charge women high prices. Do you know how hard it is for the conspirators to keep the agreement? A conspiracy to keep prices high usually falls apart because the conspirators find cheating on the deal irresistible. They lower their price or offer other inducements to help the consumer. Even OPEC, the oil cartel, breaks down all the time and prices get set by a competitive supply along with demand. And OPEC has a relatively small number of conspirators. Besides, if you're right, then someone has an incentive to open a new dry cleaning shop, price women's dry cleaning more cheaply than the conspirators, still make a hefty profit, and get a ton of business from women."

"As long as someone notices the opportunity."

"According to your view, it's widely known. Even English teachers from the Edwards School know it. There's an old joke about two economists walking down the street. One says to the other, 'Look! A $20 bill.' The other one says, 'Don't bother picking it up. If it were really there, someone would have picked it up already.'"

"I guess economics humor is a little dry."

"Yeah, just a little," Sam admitted. "But profits *do* get snapped up quickly—they're like money in the street. And the way to grab the opportunity is to figure out what customers want and provide it as cheaply as possible. And to keep your customers, you need to find ways to continually lower price and raise quality. Cheaper and better is the mantra of modern business. Look at straws."

"Straws?"

"You know, drinking straws. A paper straw works fine. But even for a product as trivial as a straw, it gets improved. You can have paper or plastic. You can have it in color or with stripes. You can pay a little bit more and get it with a bend built in. You can have it with a little spoon on the end. Or take floss. You can have floss with mint, without mint, waxed or unwaxed, with Gortex or fruit-flavored, in a clear dispenser or solid. No one sits still. People are constantly trying to find ways to make your life better. Every possible niche of consumer taste gets explored."

"I don't know. It seems trivial. Do we need more than one kind of straw or floss?"

"I can't answer that question, any more than I can tell you if we need more than one kind of cell phone or one kind of cancer treatment or one kind of shirt or one kind of cereal. Trivial or sublime, you can no more stop the marketplace from filling every obscure niche of consumer desire than you can stop the rain forest from blossoming in every direction. Does a rain forest really need more than ten kinds of flowers? Does every square inch need to be alive with life? Can't some of it be left alone? In the rain forest, species compete for sunlight and moisture and nutrients. The same thing is going on in the marketplace. In the marketplace, the competition is over customers—the sunlight that catches the attention of the innovator. Profits are the reward for discovery. Then competition comes along and drives down prices and profits get smaller. Dry cleaning isn't exactly a new market. If there were a lot of money to be made by offering women dry cleaning at lower prices, my guess is that someone would have done it already. Do you like tea?"

"Sure."

"Do you think we need more than one type of hot beverage with and without caffeine? You weren't even content to order coffee. You're having a skim latte. Imagine coping with a world of tea and only tea."

"I confess," Laura said laughing. "I usually prefer coffee."

"And you shall have it, in all its varieties and flavors if the decision is left to the marketplace."

"It's a bit of an addiction. I guess that makes me a slave to the diversity produced by the market."

Sam smiled. A few more customers had come in while they had been talking. The tables began to fill up. Sam was glad to be sitting at the window. He liked the commotion of the street as a backdrop to their conversation.

"There are worse forms of slavery," he said.

"But if cheaper and better is the norm," Laura asked, "why do things keep getting more expensive? Competition doesn't seem to be working."

"The effects are masked by inflation. Prices were a lot lower 50 or 100 years ago, but incomes were a lot lower too. To see how well we're being served by the marketplace, you have to take out the impact of inflation on both."

"And what do you find?"

"A school teacher a hundred years ago made a little over $300 a year. She—"

"Ouch. And I thought I was underpaid."

"She also faced lower prices. Eggs were only 20¢ a dozen

back then. But eggs are cheaper in a real sense when they're $1 a dozen and you make $26,000 a year. If you make that comparison across a wide range of goods, your standard of living is many times higher than your 1900 or 1950 counterparts. And that comparison wildly understates the real impact of economic innovation—you enjoy goods and services that they couldn't have imagined—your mint-flavored floss, skim latte, the car you drive, your computer, the Internet, antibiotics, and the other incredible advances in medical care. All those changes come courtesy of the marketplace and competition. And one thing I'm pretty sure of."

"What's that?"

"We know a school teacher of 1900 was never exploited by high prices for women's dry cleaning—she almost certainly washed her shirts by hand."

Laura laughed. She looked out the window and noticed that the sidewalks were a little busier than before. She fought off an urge to look at her watch—she could probably spare a few more minutes. She was enjoying the conversation and something was still bothering her about Sam's argument.

"OK," she asked, "then what about a business that has no competitors? Surely you believe in protecting the consumer from a monopolist."

"Monopoly is rare and unnatural. Look at what a farmer has to do to keep a cornfield free of competition from other plants. It's the same in business. Every business has competitors. Even when they don't know it. Ever hear of Keuffel and Esser?"

"Sounds like a law firm."

"They made slide rules."

Laura looked puzzled.

"They disappeared before our time," Sam explained. "My dad had one. They were primitive devices for multiplying numbers, figuring out cube roots and other calculations. Keuffel and Esser made the best ones. Had a huge market share. In 1967, Keuffel and Esser commissioned a study of what the world would be like in the year 2067. The study failed to foresee a critical event that was only five years away: the invention of the pocket calculator. An invention that would destroy the slide rule forever. Competition can come from anywhere. That's why Bill Gates, Microsoft's founder, sleeps poorly."

"I find that hard to believe, Sam. Now there's a guy who has control over a market."

"But Bill Gates sleeps poorly because he knows that if he doesn't continue to innovate, he'll end up like Keuffel and Esser. Maybe some merger will knock him off. Or another operating system. Or a whole new method of computing."

"So what should Bill Gates do?"

"What he *shouldn't* do is spend a lot of time figuring out how to gouge customers. That will only hasten the growth of future competitors. He should serve the customer. And it's the profit motive that drives him to do so."

"I don't know, Sam. You make business sound like some civilized game of cricket played by men dressed in white, speaking in English accents. At the end of the match, both teams cheerfully hoist the referee, otherwise known as the consumer, onto their shoulders while singing 'For he's a jolly good fellow.' I see a different, grubbier struggle, more like rugby where the consumer is often ground into the mud."

"OK. Suppose through some bizarre, barely imaginable chain of events you found yourself wallowing in the grubby world of business. Would you want your employees to be ruthless or loving?"

Laura laughed softly at the thought of running a business.

"Ever stay in a Ritz-Carlton?" Sam asked before she could answer.

"Once, with my parents, I think it was Atlanta."

"Do you know the Ritz-Carlton's motto?"

Laura rolled her eyes. "Come on, Sam. How would I know their motto?"

"Sorry. I use it as an example in class all the time so I forget that it's not on the tip of everyone's tongue. Their motto is 'The highest price and the greatest profit.'"

"You're kidding."

"Of course I am. That's their *secret* motto. They use it around the boardroom when they make their plans to exploit customers. Kidding again. Their actual motto is 'Ladies and gentlemen serving ladies and gentlemen.'"

"That's pretty elegant for a motto."

"It's not exactly an invitation to cut corners or skimp on service. Here's another example that I happen to have here in my wallet."

"In your wallet?"

"I'm a weirdo. Or haven't you been paying attention?" Sam unfolded a piece of paper from his wallet. "Actually I'm using it in class this week so I've got it with me. It's an old quote from an executive at Merck, one of the world's great pharmaceutical companies. 'We try to remember that medicine is for the patient.

We try never to forget that medicine is for the people. It is not for the profits. The profits follow, and if we have remembered that, they have never failed to appear. The better we have remembered that, the larger they have been.' Isn't it strange? If you focus too much on the bottom line, you're less likely to succeed. Successful companies—companies like Wal-Mart or Southwest Airlines or FedEx or Merck—bring quality products, extraordinary service and low prices to the customer. That is how they have become successful. And they have forced their competitors to try and match their performance."

"Are you telling me that the CEOs of those companies aren't interested in making money?"

"No, I think they like money as much as the rest of us. But greed isn't the key to success. Who do you think would do a better job of serving the customer? A greedy selfish pig who pretends to care about others, or a genuinely nice person who treats customers well with sincerity?"

"That's absurd, Sam. Nice people don't finish first in business."

"I'm not saying that the gentle and caring people of the world are found at the top of the modern corporation. But the scum of the earth can't make it to the top either. Do you remember asking me about that poster I have of 'It's a Wonderful Life'?"

"Sure. We were on the Metro."

"I love that movie because it presents two caricatured views of business. You have Jimmy Stewart as George Bailey who would never make a business decision that would hurt one of his customers. Then you have Lionel Barrymore as Mr. Potter who enjoys repossessing a house and delights in throwing the residents out into the street. In the movie, George is the hero. But he's probably a lousy businessman."

"What's the matter—too nice a guy?"

"No. He's a lousy businessman because he doesn't seem to realize that profit keeps a business alive. Without it, you're bankrupt and you can't help your customers or your employees. Potter is also a lousy businessman. He's a vicious and selfish man who would repel customers and employees. In the real world, you need a mix of Potter's intensity and George's goodness. Besides, I have a good cry every time I see it."

"Hmm. I thought you had to have your tear ducts surgically removed before you could get your economics degree. I doubt goodness counts for much of anything in the boardroom or in the marketplace."

"But it does. Meaning what you say, keeping your word, and serving others without resentment are probably more valuable in the business world than elsewhere. Take a look at the best-selling business books. They aren't about manipulating the customer or exploiting employees. They're often about integrity. Leadership. Motivation. Many of them apply religious principles to business."

"I find that hard to believe, but to be honest, I have a confession to make. I'm glad you're sitting down—this will shock you. I don't read too many business books."

"Most English teachers don't. But that means you're probably getting your perspective on business from a Dickens novel or Hollywood or a television show. So when you think of business, you see smokestacks belching out poison into the air. You see a sinister businessman, surrounded by bags of money, rubbing his hands together in glee as he plots to exploit his customers in new and exciting ways. In popular culture, business is always portrayed as monstrous because that's what sells. People like feeling victimized so that they can hate their oppressor. But monsters don't often succeed in business. The sweeter competitor offering good service and low prices is a better bet. There's an invisible heart at the core of the marketplace, serving the customer and doing it joyously. Can I get you a refill?"

"Thanks. Decaf this time. If the choice is available."

"Of course, madame," Sam said, standing up and nodding politely in mock servitude. "Capitalism at your service."

While Sam went for the drinks, Laura wondered if Sam was a typical economist. She had always thought of economists as being mainly interested in money. But in Sam's world, money seemed a sideshow rather than the main event.

"Careful, it's hot," Sam said when he returned, putting Laura's drink down.

"Great. That's the way it should be."

Sam thought of saying something about lawsuits and hot coffee, but he kept quiet instead and looked out the window. It was his favorite time of day. Daylight fading, but not quite night. The streetlights just on. People hurrying home from work. Sam's hands encircled his teacup and he smiled at Laura. He looked into her eyes. All the anger was gone.

"So maybe this greed thing is a bit exaggerated," Laura said. "Then why do you play that game in your class where you dangle the dollars?"

"Some of the students think the purpose of the game is to show that greed is good. But that isn't the purpose at all. The point is to show the power of self-interest. If you knew that someone was out there dropping dollars every day, you'd spend time trying to find out where and how to get there. You'd spend time finding ways to jump higher or build something to help you reach higher. Self-interest isn't good or bad. It's a fact of life. We strive. We try to do better. We try to get ahead. It's a fundamental part of our humanity. And the marketplace channels our nature in a way that serves others. That's the lesson of Adam Smith, the author of *The Wealth of Nations*. People think he believed that greed was good. But he merely wanted to explain the power of self-interest." Sam stopped and gazed up at the ceiling, lost in thought. "What do you eat for breakfast?" he asked suddenly.

"Usually a toasted bagel," Laura answered, a bit bewildered by this turn in the conversation. She thought of glancing at the ceiling. What did Sam see up there that turned his mind to bagels?

"And where do you buy your bagels?"

"There's a little place around the corner from me. Why do you want to know?"

"Do you have any at home right now?" Sam asked, ignoring her question.

"I think I'm out, actually. I'll probably pick some up on the way home or tomorrow morning."

"Do you think you ought to call them and let them know you're coming by?"

"Why?" Laura asked, now totally at sea.

"If they don't know you're coming, maybe they won't make enough." Sam sat back in his chair, contentedly, despite the absurdity of the question.

"What are you talking about, Sam? They always have enough."

"Ever wonder why that is?" Sam asked. He leaned forward in excitement. "Do you ever go to sleep worrying that the bakers of the city won't make enough bagels for tomorrow? Never! But why not? Some mornings, you only buy one. Some mornings a dozen. Some mornings you don't buy any. Some mornings you buy three dozen because you're throwing a brunch. Isn't it amazing that all over the city, tomorrow, there will be plenty of bagels? You and your fellow bagel lovers don't have to make reservations. You just show up and there they are. Isn't it wondrous?"

Laura giggled to hear Sam expressing rapture over a bagel.

"Your bagel maker depends on a thousand unseen people to help get bagels to you—farmers and flour makers and truck drivers and the myriad of people who support them. No one coordinates the process. Washington doesn't need a bagel czar to keep them hard at work. No one needs to call the baker to get up at 3:30 in the morning to make sure the bagels are fresh. Most of us wouldn't be comfortable asking a friend to get up at 3:30 in the morning to do us a favor. But to make sure your bagel is fresh, a stranger does it voluntarily. Not out of love for you. But out of self-interest. To make sure the business survives by keeping the customer contented."

"I still think I'd rather be served by someone who's motivated by something other than self-interest."

"Self-interested doesn't mean cold-hearted or even selfish. The baker who gets up at 3:30 may be motivated by high and lofty goals. He may plan on amassing a fortune and giving it away to charity. He may be getting up early to make sure he earns enough money to afford an operation for his child or to be able to buy a nice home for his family. He may be overflowing with love for many people and many causes. But the powerful thing about the marketplace is that your baker doesn't have to be overflowing with love for *you* to treat you well. Competition combines with self-interest to serve you—without anyone being in charge. And it works so flawlessly, we never even notice it."

"I will from now on. The marketplace *is* extraordinary. But it's not flawless. There are defective products. There are dangerous products. There are products sold by slick advertising that don't live up to their hype. There are good CEOs like you say. But there are heartless ones who succeed and prosper. I don't want to get rid of the marketplace. I just want to make it better."

"And I think it's perfect."

"Perfect? You're joking, right?"

"Not really. You can have a perfect system with imperfect outcomes. I'm willing to tolerate that degree of imperfection because when you tamper with a complex system, you often make things worse. That's why so much regulation often hurts the people we're trying to help. It's like saying I think the rain forest doesn't make enough yellow flowers. You can artificially induce the rain forest to make more yellow flowers. But they may be scrawnier or less healthy. And you will have other unseen effects that you may not like. Because you have more yellow flowers, you may end up with less red ones that some lizard or frog or butterfly depends on. I'd rather rely on competition to discipline imperfection."

"I'm more optimistic about regulation. I think we can take what's good about the marketplace and improve it."

"Maybe. But I doubt it. Look how the Internet has evolved. Problems come along—problems with kids seeing inappropriate stuff, problems with keeping financial transactions secure. Then entrepreneurs find ways to solve those problems. And they don't just find one way. They find lots of ways that give consumers choice. The solutions aren't perfect. Some kids still see things their parents would keep from them and credit card info still gets stolen. But if the government stepped in to make it even better, do you think the Internet would be where it is now? Leave it alone and it flourishes."

Laura thought for a moment.

"You like the rain forest," she said. "I like an English garden. You like the wild look and I'm in favor of a little bit of pruning. If you're going to have a garden, I think you need a gardener. Or maybe a team of gardeners."

"If you can tell me how to take mere mortals and make them omniscient and incorruptible gardeners, I'm open to the suggestion."

"I'll give you this." Laura stopped and leaned forward, beaming at Sam. "I've almost forgotten about the price of this dry cleaning. So if competition does such a good job of protecting the consumer, why do women pay more than men?"

"Just guessing, but women's blouses are probably more costly to clean than men's shirts and the higher price reflects the cost."

"How can that be? Don't they get cleaned in the same place with the same materials?"

"Maybe women's blouses take longer to clean. They've got all those what-do-you-call-'ems."

"Do you mean darts, Mr. Armani?"

"You tell me. Fashion's not my field. But if women's blouses take longer to clean, dry cleaners will have to charge more to cover the cost. Whatever the reason, my guess is that if you opened a dry cleaner that charged the same prices for women's blouses and men's dress shirts, you'd lose money. If you raised the prices on men's shirts to that of women's, you'd lose business to lower-priced competitors. If you lowered the prices you charged women, my guess is you couldn't cover your costs."

"I don't believe it," said Laura.

"Fair enough. Let's gather some data."

Laura looked at Sam, puzzled. She scooped up her valuable dry cleaning and followed Sam out into the night, wondering where they were headed. With the sun down, the temperature had dropped noticeably. Laura wished she were wearing a thicker sweater. She gave a short involuntary shiver. Sam took off his jacket and draped it over her shoulders as they walked.

"Hey, thanks. Are you OK?"

"I'm fine." Sam reassured her, "We're not going far."

They headed back across the street and up the block. They stood in front of Capitol Cleaners.

"Now what?" Laura asked.

"The horse's mouth. Here we are," Sam said, as the bell over the door jangled at their entrance. "Hello, Mrs. Williams."

Mrs. Williams had been at the counter of Capitol Cleaning long before Sam had been coming there. The store was her fiefdom and she stood proudly behind the counter, her gray hair neatly pinned up. She peered up at Sam through thick spectacles.

"Hello, Mr. Gordon," she said, smiling in greeting as she did with all her customers. "And Ms. Silver," she added in a what-have-we-here voice.

"You don't charge the same price for women's blouses as you do for men's shirts," Sam said. "Any idea why that is?"

Mrs. Williams looked relieved. She had worried for a moment that Laura had been dissatisfied in some way with her newly cleaned blouses.

"Women's shirts are smaller than men's," she said. "They don't fit on the machine that we use for men's shirts, so they have to be done by hand. It takes longer that way, so we charge more. We also charge more for cleaning children's shirts for the same reason. Why do you ask?"

"I'm thinking of opening a competing store across the street," Sam answered, winking at Mrs. Williams. "I was looking for a strategy to undercut your prices. I see I'll have to come up with something else. Thanks for your time."

Sam and Laura stepped outside. Sam wanted to declare victory but held his tongue.

"OK," Laura said finally. "You were right and I was wrong. It's hard to believe dry cleaners are making a killing by exploiting women and *children*."

"Don't give up so soon," Sam said. "Maybe they overcharge on children's clothes to cover up their sexist pricing strategy. Maybe it does cost more to clean women's blouses but not enough to justify the price. Besides, your fallback position can be that the makers of the dry cleaning machines are in on the conspiracy and refuse to design and manufacture a machine for smaller-sized shirts. Though maybe there just aren't enough women's shirts that get dry-cleaned to make it profitable. But cheer up. Mrs. Williams knows a lot of my intimate secrets. She knows when I splatter food on my shirts, she knows that I buy inexpensive pens that leak, and she knows all kinds of other marginalia about my life via my clothes. Now she knows I just spent time with one of her customers, a fact that seemed to be of great interest to her. But she may not know the real reason for why shirts are priced the way they are. She's just a single data point, as we say in economics. Let's take our classes on a field trip and gather some real evidence, first-hand."

"Fun idea," Laura said, both surprised and glad that Sam was taking up her side rather than exulting in triumph. "Economics in everyday life. But I doubt I can justify bringing my English class on a field trip to a dry cleaner."

"Didn't Dickens write about sweatshops and the oppression of the working class?"

"I still think it's a stretch."

"I suppose. Hey, you doing anything for dinner?"

Laura looked at her watch and shook her head. "I'd love to but I've got too much work. Maybe another time. Thanks for the loaner," she said, returning his coat.

Despite the chill in the air, Sam decided to walk down Connecticut to his apartment off Dupont Circle rather than take the Metro. It had been a friendly enough conversation, but he worried about whether Laura's workload was the real reason she had declined his dinner invitation. He decided it would be a good idea to chat with Laura about something other than economics. But what could it possibly be?

Eight MAGIC FINGERS

The few HealthNet employees who make their way into Charles Krauss's presence have various names for the three women who work in his suite. Some call them the Harpies. Some call them Charlie's Angels. But everyone uses the same name for the receptionist who sits in the open area where guests wait before seeing Krauss. She is known as Cerberus, after the three-headed dog in Greek mythology who guarded the entrance to Hell.

The Cerberus position has high turnover and highly variable productivity. Cerberus has a narrow set of responsibilities. She answers the phone for the entire suite and knows to tell all callers for Mr. Krauss that he is in a meeting and will return the call at his convenience. She makes the coffee. She does the occasional copying job in the glassed-in alcove next to her desk. And she is the ornament for guests to admire when are waiting to see Krauss. The other two women in the suite are highly skilled executive assistants who have been with Krauss for years.

The current Cerberus is Heather Hathaway, a young woman from San Diego who had worked on Capitol Hill as a low-level staffer for a member of Congress from California. Like the previous occupants of the position, she is tall, blond, and physically fit. Today, she sits at her desk outside of Krauss's office thinking about the woman in Ohio she saw on the news last night. She is thinking of the children who stood by the woman's side. The innocence of their faces. Their blissful ignorance of the future. She's still angry to think that she works for a company that could do that to people. Is there a way to strike back? Maybe here in the office, before she quits her job, there is an opportunity to accomplish something.

The buzzing of the intercom interrupts her reverie.

"Yes, Mr. Krauss?"

"Miss Hathaway. Please bring me the magic fingers."

The magic fingers is Krauss's phrase for the portable document shredder. Heather often does the shredding herself at the portable shredder next to the copying machine. But on occasion, Krauss asks to do the task himself and has Heather bring the shredder into his office. Heather has always wondered why Krauss refuses to delegate some of the shredding. He couldn't enjoy shredding documents. Surely he is hiding something.

Heather Hathaway carries the shredder into Krauss's office. On Krauss's desk stands a stack of papers, a tidy white island on the inky sea of his desk. Heather glances over at the clock. It is almost eleven. Her heart begins to pound. This may be her chance.

"You are looking lovely today," he says, laying his hand on her arm as she puts the shredder next to his chair. He smiles at her.

She escapes his grasp and returns to the desk out front. Now she watches the clock. It is just before 11:00. Krauss always smokes a cigarette at 11:00 sharp. Rather than smoke in his office, he exits through a private door off of his office onto the courtyard with the Japanese garden. This is one of Krauss's few concessions to the attitudes of the day. He doesn't care about offending his visitors with second-hand smoke, but it bothers him that they might think a CEO of a health company is a smoker only because he lacks the discipline to quit.

Sure enough, at 11:00, Heather hears Krauss get up from his desk and head out into the courtyard for his nicotine fix. Marge, the executive assistant with the office right next to Krauss's, can see the courtyard from her window. Heather buzzes her on the intercom.

"Marge? Heather."

"Hey."

"Mr. Krauss just stepped out for his morning cigarette, and—"

"I see him."

"I've got some copying to do, and Krauss hates it when I use the machine for personal stuff. You know how he likes to pop into the copying alcove and keep an eye on things. Will you buzz me when you see him heading back inside?"

"Sure, dear."

"I owe you one."

Heather takes a deep breath. The phone is quiet. No visitors are expected. She hurries from behind her desk and enters Krauss's office. The door to the courtyard stands open.

She exults to see that a significant stack of the papers on Krauss's desk remain unshredded. Heather never thought she would be grateful for the addictive power of nicotine. She grabs a fistful of paper, a good two or three inches and races out to the copier. A quick moment of indecision. Should she put the whole stack in the feeder or look to see which pages might be important? She has little time. Krauss will not be long. In a show of control, he never smokes much more than half of his cigarette.

What to do? Heather feels sweat dampening her underarms. Hell, she thinks. Let's go all the way. Just don't jam on me. She drops the entire stack into the feeder and watches anxiously as the machine methodically spits out page after page. It seems like an eternity, but finally it is done. She stuffs the copies into her oversized purse underneath her desk and sprints toward Krauss's office with the originals. As she enters the office, she can hear the intercom at her desk buzzing behind her. Marge! It's going to be close.

She just has time to arrange the pile of originals on Krauss's desk and slip back through the door to the reception area. When

Krauss buzzes her to come in and reclaim the shredder, he seems to suspect nothing.

At home that night, Heather looks over the fruits of her courage. Long columns of numbers and terms she does not recognize. She has no idea whether her gamble has any value or likely pay-off. Maybe someone else will be able to figure if the numbers mean anything. All she knows is that Krauss must have had a reason for wanting them destroyed in private. That should be good enough. She has done what she can.

She dials 1-800-CALL-OCR.

"You have reached the hotline for the Office of Corporate Responsibility. If you would like to leave a voice message please wait until the beep. Make sure to identify the name of the company or organization and as much detail as possible about the events or actions that you are reporting. If you have printed materials, you may send them to P.O. Box 5273, Washington, DC, 20580. Thank you for your cooperation."

Heather writes down the address. She takes the copies she made earlier in the day, attaches a brief note on a plain white sheet of paper, and slides everything into a manila envelope. The next day, she goes to the post office near her apartment and sends them to the OCR.

∞

Two days later, Erica Baldwin sits at her desk and opens the manila envelope that Heather Hathaway has sent. On top of a stack of papers is a note—"Someone at HealthNet wanted these destroyed." And then on the next line, "A friend at HealthNet."

Erica stares at the long columns of numbers. What do they mean? The note only suggests that the numbers have something to say. Something to say about the mystery at the heart of the HealthNet investigation, the final piece of the case that will pull everything together. Then she remembers a Paul Simon song from years before, a song about numbers. It wasn't a hit, but it has always been one of her favorite songs.

I will love you innumerably,
You can count on my word.
When times are mysterious,
Serious numbers will always be heard.

Humming the tune, she clears a space on her cluttered desk and lays the papers down. She stares at the neat numbers in their clean columns and waits for inspiration.

Nine THE SIREN'S CALL

It was lunchtime on a Friday afternoon in early March when Laura stopped by the administrative office of the Edwards School to pick up her paycheck. The term was in full swing and it had been a long month. She was looking forward to the weekend. Lois McCarthy, the Principal's secretary who handled the paychecks, was not at her desk.

"Back in a minute" read the post-it note hanging from the front of the desk. As Laura turned to leave, her eyes caught sight of a thick file folder there with Sam Gordon's name on it. She had heard the rumors that Sam was in some sort of trouble. She had an overwhelming desire to pick up the folder, but thought better of it. Then she saw the memo lying next to the folder. Her eyes caught the boldface words "Decision by the Board" and "Opportunity for Appeal" just as Lois returned.

Laura went by the faculty lounge and grabbed her lunch of yogurt and an apple. "Opportunity for Appeal" sounded ominous. So maybe Sam really was under threat of dismissal. The thought disturbed her more than she expected. He was peculiar. His perspective on life was so different from hers. But because of that she enjoyed their encounters. On top of everything, he seemed to be a good guy. It seemed hard to believe that he could face dismissal. What could he have done? Did an appeal leave any hope that Sam could salvage his job?

It was a gorgeous day for March. Laura decided to eat outside in the courtyard of the school. The students and faculty shared the courtyard for lunch and social events. It was landscaped with flowers and small trees around a circular brick patio. The patio was ringed with benches. On one of these benches, Sam Gordon was sitting placidly, eating a granola bar and reading a book.

"May I join you?" Laura asked.

"Sure," Sam said, frantically searching his mind for a topic of conversation other than economics or public policy. He drew a blank.

"So what's your next class?" he asked, hoping to find some material there.

"It's a senior poetry elective. Mostly nineteenth-century British poets."

Not my best field, Sam thought. But he pushed onward.

"What are you covering today?" he asked.

"'Ulysses,' by Tennyson. Ever read it?"

"Can't say that I have. Is it good?"

"No, it's terrible. Of course it's good. I wouldn't have assigned it if it weren't good. But it's not just good in the sense of being good poetry. It's just plain good."

"Would you read some of it to me?"

Laura wasn't exactly comfortable giving a dramatic reading of "Ulysses" to Sam Gordon. She looked around. Nobody was paying attention to them. Some students sat in a corner of the courtyard listening to a student finger-pick a guitar. A few faculty sat on the benches. No one seemed within earshot. Why not, she thought. Sam could probably use a boost and Tennyson's "Ulysses" was way up there in the boosting department.

"I'll read you the end. It's magnificent. If you like it, you can go back on your own and read the beginning."

"Great. Fire away," Sam said.

"First some background. You know about Ulysses, right? A.k.a. Odysseus. Fights in the Trojan War for ten years. Then ten more years of scrapes and adventures. Finally, he returns home. He's scared. Afraid of what he'll find. Has Penelope been faithful?"

"The wife?"

"You got it."

"And?"

"Not to worry. She did have boatloads of suitors. You can imagine that the wife of Ulysses would draw a crowd while he was away. While her suitors wooed her, she knitted. And she promised her suitors an answer as soon as she finished her knitting. Each night she would unravel that day's knitting. That was how she kept putting off the propositions."

"She must have been some woman," Sam said.

"Undoubtedly. Ulysses finally returns home disguised as a beggar. The suitors are camped out at his house, still seeking Penelope's hand. Ulysses devises a plan to rout the suitors. It works. He and Penelope are reunited. They embrace and—"

"Fade out."

"Not quite. That's not what Tennyson wants to write about. That's too easy. He writes about the last years. The glow of that reunion has faded. Ulysses is an old man. Carrying out the day-to-day tasks of being king. Wondering if he has lived his life well. The once great warrior and sailor facing the unpleasantness of a diminished future. Infirmity. Death. This is where Tennyson picks up the story."

"Sounds terribly depressing."

"Much of the poem has a melancholy tone. But Tennyson ends it on a different note. The poem is written in the first person. Ulysses is talking. He wonders whether he might gather his mariners for one last voyage of courage. A voyage of almost unimaginable grandeur. Made much more grand by the age of the voyagers."

"Kind of like a great athlete in the twilight of his career, pinch-hitting in the World Series."

"That's great. I'll use it in class."

"But the old guy usually pops out to the catcher in foul territory."

"Right. But remember this is an old man's imaginings of what the future could hold. And what Tennyson is saying—at least I believe what Tennyson is saying—is that it's OK to fail when your skills have faded and the spotlight is on you. What's really important is still having enough fire in the belly to even consider getting into the arena at all."

"I like that," Sam said. What he really liked, though, was sitting outside on a March day just warm enough to sit outside and talking to Laura Silver about something other than wages or prices.

"There's one more thing you need to know," she continued. "Ulysses, when he speaks, refers to the Happy Isles. According to Greek mythology, this was Elysium, the opposite of Hades, or Hell. Bad folks went to Hades. Good people went to the Happy Isles."

"Was there a Cerberus at the Happy Isles or only one in Hades?"

"Cerberus! How do you know about Cerberus?" asked Laura.

"Pretty obscure isn't it? I don't know. It just popped into my head. My Dad used to read me Greek mythology when I was a kid. I guess a three-headed dog caught my imagination. Anyway, go ahead."

Laura paused. She looked around to make sure that they were still unnoticed. Then she took a breath and began.

Death closes all; but something ere the end,
Some work of noble note, may yet be done
Not unbecoming men that strove with Gods.
The lights begin to twinkle from the rocks;

The long day wanes; the slow moon climbs; the deep
Moans round with many voices.

"That's Tennyson's way of describing all the different
sounds of the ocean. Now Ulysses speaks to his friends who are
still alive and invites them to join him on a last great voyage."

Come, my friends.
'Tis not too late to seek a newer world.
Push off, and sitting well in order smite
The sounding furrows; for my purpose holds
To sail beyond the sunset, and the baths
Of all the western stars, until I die.
It may be that the gulfs will wash us down;
It may be we shall touch the Happy Isles,
And see the great Achilles whom we knew.

Sam noticed that Laura was no longer reading but reciting
from memory, eyes closed, the lines of poetry coursing through
her with the rhythm of the waves. Sam wanted to look away
because of the intensity of her delivery. But he could not tear his
glance away from the purity of her face as the words poured out
of her.

Tho' much is taken, much abides; and tho'
We are not now that strength which in old days
Moved earth and heaven, that which we are, we are,—
One equal temper of heroic hearts,

Made weak by time and fate, but strong in will
To strive, to seek, to find, and not to yield.

Laura's words hovered in the air like the last note of a symphony before the audience begins to applaud. Sam wanted to tell her how the words filled his heart, but he was afraid to break the spell she had cast. Laura also felt it. It made her uncomfortable. What was she doing using these words from a century ago to charm this peculiar python from the world of economics?

"Iambic pentameter," she finally said, shaking her head in amazement.

"You're what?" asked Sam.

"Iambic pentameter. It's jargon for the type of rhythm in the poem. It gives the words such power."

"Can I hear the last two lines again?"

Laura hesitated. But she did it anyway.

"That last bit would make a magnificent credo," said Sam.

"Oh yes," Laura said. She saw a way to resolve the tension from the intimacy she had created.

"It's just a tad more elegant than 'Ladies and gentlemen serving ladies and gentlemen,'" she said.

"Hey, you remembered!"

"I did. I was paying attention. But don't confuse a good memory with admitting defeat. I still think companies should pay a price when they abuse their customers."

But they do, Sam wanted to say. Unhappy customers don't come back and neither do the friends they tell. But he didn't want to ruin the mood. He was so proud of having a conversation on poetry. He wasn't going to spoil it.

"Why, look at the time," Sam said with mock alarm. "And you haven't even had a chance to eat. I have to run anyway. I've got a meeting with good ol' Principal Harkin. We can talk about corporate responsibility another time."

The mention of Principal Harkin reminded her of that thick folder in the Principal's office with Sam's name on it. He was probably having a tough time and a feeling of sympathy surged through her.

"Hey, Sam. I know it's short notice, but are you doing anything Saturday night? There's a dinner party at my folks' place in Georgetown. Would you like to come?"

Sam's face lit up.

"I'd love to. Should I wear a coat and tie?"

A straitjacket might be more appropriate attire if you start talking politics with my family, thought Laura. Oh well. The deed was done.

"Whatever you like. I'll put a note in your mail slot with directions."

Of course it will be OK, Laura thought to herself. What could go wrong? Sam could get into an argument about corporate responsibility and government intervention. But how bad could that be?

Ten DOWN AND DIRTY

George Sutherland rubs his eyes and goes over to the rusty basin in the corner of his motel room in hopes of finding a little bit of hot water this morning. He is sick of Mexico. Sick of the dirt, sick of his job, and sick with longing for his wife and children back in Ohio. He has been in Mexico for almost four months, two months overseeing the construction of the HealthNet factory that has taken the place of the one in Matalon and two months making sure everything is running smoothly. In a week he will turn the plant over to the new permanent manager.

George throws on the same clothes he wore yesterday and goes out to the pickup truck. The engine hesitates, no more eager than George to face another day, but George nurses it to life. He heads for the airstrip on the edge of town.

Along the way he passes a jumble of corrugated tin shacks in an open field. A goat and a pair of chickens wander here and there among half-naked children. The children hurry to the side of the road and wave wildly. George grins in response and waves back.

He is picking up two VIPs from corporate headquarters in Virginia, coming in this morning. There is no airport, just a small airstrip for private planes. George parks the truck by the chain-link fence surrounding the airstrip and waits. His mind is a blank. He just wants to get this tour of duty over with, collect his money and head back to Ohio. He passes the time staring off into the distance, thinking about his wife and kids. After about thirty minutes, a small jet touches down. It coasts to a stop across from George's truck. The plane's door opens and two people clamber out.

The first is a young man, much younger than George had expected. He can't be more than thirty-five. He wears a suit. The woman who steps down after him is even younger, maybe thirty, tops. She is dressed casually in chinos, a simple white T-shirt, and a photographer's vest. George waves to them and catches their attention. They head his way.

"George Sutherland, Interim Plant Manager. Welcome to Mexico," he says.

The young man hesitates. George smiles. He must have expected a more elegant greeting party.

"Hello," says the young man finally, extending a hand in greeting. "Rob Blankenship, Director of Public Relations, HealthNet. And this is Alice—she's a photographer."

Alice who? George thinks, wondering at the man's rudeness. He suspects this is Blankenship's first trip to Mexico. In addition to the expensive suit he wears, he carries an overnighter of buttery leather that must be worth a month's wages for most Mexicans.

Blankenship is not happy climbing into a very dusty pickup truck in his nice suit. Alice is distracted—her eyes search the landscape, seeing it for the first time. She wears a big Nikon around her neck and carries a large bag full of more equipment. They climb into the truck. Both passengers carry their bags on their laps. Blankenship does not want his $300 leather bag to bounce around in the back. Alice is concerned for her cameras.

"Sorry about the truck," George says. "This is about as clean as you can get anything down here."

"So how is the plant coming along?" Blankenship asks. He does not want to think about the truck.

"It's fine. Everything is just about in place. On schedule. You'll get some good pictures."

"They're for our annual report. I also need some background for a press release now that the plant is operational with all of the bugs worked out."

George grimaces. The bugs have been worked out from day one.

"Alice here is one of our best freelancers," Blankenship continues. "She can make a factory look like a cathedral. Or whatever you want. We had a plant in—"

"Stop the truck!" Alice shouts suddenly.

George screeches to a stop. He sees nothing. Alice, who sits at the window, is out of the truck in a flash. She is heading for the jumble of huts, goats and kids that George passed on the way to the airport. The kids swarm around her. A goat tries to nuzzle his way to the center. When the kids discover that she wants to take their picture, they become even more animated. It takes Alice a while to calm them down so that she can start shooting.

"Artists," Blankenship laughs. "Only an artist can find poverty picturesque. So these are the homeless?" he asks.

"I'm afraid not." George answers patiently. "This is where most of our workers live. That woman over there hanging out laundry is the wife of one of our supervisors."

Blankenship is stunned into silence. George can't decide who he feels sorrier for, the workers back in Ohio who have been replaced by the parents of these kids, or the Mexicans who are working twelve hours a day for a fraction of what his friends back in Ohio used to make.

"People here make about $8 a day," George continues. "A supervisor might make $10. That comes out to a little more than $2,000 a year. You can't afford much of a mortgage on that when you have six kids."

"I knew we moved this plant here to save money. I just never realized how the people here live."

"That's how they live." And that's how they die, George thinks to himself.

The two men sit in silence in the dusty cab.

A few minutes later, Alice climbs back into the cab, shaking her head in amazement. "Those children have beautiful faces. So innocent, yet so—. . ." She searches for the word.

"I don't care about those kids, Alice," Blankenship interrupts. "Give me that film."

"What?"

"Some of those families are HealthNet employees. Just give me the film. We don't need those pictures turning up somewhere they don't belong by mistake. Just give me the film."

Alice's shoulders slump. She opens the back of the camera and gives him the film. Blankenship pulls the film out from the canister exposing it to the air. The three ride on in silence for the ten minutes it takes to get to the factory.

"This looks like a perfect replica of the plant in Matalon," Blankenship says cheerily as George pulls into the parking lot.

"From the outside. Inside it's a little, well, simpler."

"What do you mean?"

"There's none of the safety equipment we have back in the plant there. There's no OSHA to force us to put it in. Out here, if we have a higher accident rate, there are no worker's comp payments to worry about." George tries to say it matter-of-factly but he's angry with the way things are run.

Blankenship hears it. He reddens slightly but says nothing. While Blankenship goes off to find a phone to check his voice mail back in Virginia, George takes Alice to the main floor of the factory. She flits from place to place like a small bird, full of nervous energy, looking for the right angles. George envies her vision. He can't understand what she's doing working for HealthNet. Everyone makes compromises, he guesses.

"Let me know if I can help you with anything," he offers. "I'm sorry about your pictures back there."

"That's OK. Blankenship isn't just a jerk. He's also a fool. That camera he took the film from was the *second* one I had used, with a different lens. There are plenty of good shots on a roll of film in my first camera back in my bag. He missed those."

"Could you do me a favor? Can you make a set for me?" He stopped and took out his wallet. "Here's my card with my home address back in Ohio. Can you send me a set? And tell me how I can get in touch with you back in the States?"

"Sure. You like pictures of kids and goats?" Alice smiles.

"Yeah. Kids and goats. Thanks."

The rest of the day seems endless. Alice explores the factory while George spends the day taking care of Blankenship, giving him information about the factory and making sure he stays happy. George almost feels sorry for him. Blankenship has a constant need to assert his authority. Maybe he has so little back in Virginia, coming to Mexico gives him a chance to bully people. George doesn't care. He just wants to get rid of him. There is only another week of work here before he is finished and can return to the States.

Finally George takes his guests back to the airstrip where pilot and plane are dutifully waiting. Then he returns to the plant. The sun is almost on the horizon. Shadows dapple his desk, but he leaves the lights off. He picks up the phone and dials home to his wife Cathy in Ohio. He tells her about the tribulations of the day, playing host to the young executive from Virginia. As the sun goes down, the Mexican countryside beyond the window blurs and softens. George asks about the kids.

"They're fine," she answers.

There is something in her voice, some hesitation that alerts him.

"What's wrong?" George asks.

"Really, they're fine."

"Come on, Cathy. Tell me what's going on. I need to hear about them. I want to help."

"They're OK. They're just having a tough time in school. You know how kids are."

"What are they saying?"

"Oh, George I don't know exactly, you know how kids talk. They—"

"What are they saying, Cathy?" George finds his voice rising despite his efforts.

"They're saying their Dad's a traitor. You know what a union town Matalon is." Cathy waits for the explosion. But it doesn't come.

"Do you remember the first time you saw 'The Bridge Over the River Kwai?'" he says quietly.

"Sure." She has no idea where this is heading but she is relieved that George is calm.

"I do too. I don't know why I remember, but I saw it at the drive-in."

"Hey! Who'd you go with?"

"Relax. I was only eleven. I was with my folks. So I actually saw the movie."

She laughs.

"It's always been one of my favorites," he continues. George is sitting in the dark now, the office shrouded in shadows. The darkness has closed the distance between them. He has almost forgotten that he is in Mexico and that his wife is a few thousand miles away to the north and east. "Alec Guiness, the British officer, cooperates with his Japanese captors in building a bridge. While he knows that the Japanese are the enemy, he sees the building of the bridge as a way to restore the morale of his men. When I took this job in Mexico I knew I might have regrets. But I took it for us. We needed the money. It's that simple. I also thought it would be good for my morale to stay busy. And it's only temporary. But maybe I've just been fooling myself. I feel like Alec Guiness at the end of that movie. I'm a collaborator with the enemy. I feel dirty. I—"

"Oh, honey. You didn't have a choice. We've got a mortgage to pay. And mouths to feed. The other people at the plant wouldn't have turned it down either. We were lucky. But you didn't shut down the plant here. HealthNet did. And no one here in town could have started up that new plant there. Would you feel better if they gave the job to a stranger and we were going hungry?"

"I know you're right. But I still feel bad about it. And I'm sorry to put you through all of this. I just pray something turns up soon that's permanent."

"Amen."

"Any new mail?"

"No, honey, nothing that matters."

George has sent out forty letters to potential employers. Most have been answered with a brief form letter thanking him for sending his resume and letting him know that he will hear from them if something turns up.

"I know you'd have told me already. I have to ask. I can't help it. I'm sorry. So how's the town doing?" George asks.

"Awful. Not many people have found work. Soon people are going to start running out of money. Ed's Appliance Store went broke last week. Nobody is going to be buying a new television for a while. Even Circuit City might be pulling out, they say."

"You're kidding!"

"Nope. And I ran into Susie at the grocery yesterday. She says Jack hasn't sold five cars this month. They're on their last legs. And that's the best dealer in town. You can imagine what the others are doing. The town is falling apart, George. It's falling apart."

"There ought to be a law. But there isn't. So we have to do the best we can. Don't worry Cathy. We'll make it somehow. And the town will too."

"I love you, George."

"I love you too, Cathy. I'll talk to you soon."

He lays the phone on its cradle and sits in the dark for a few moments, thinking about his wife, his kids, his town. Finally, he rouses himself out of the darkness and locks up the factory for the night. He didn't tell his wife that part of his guilt comes from his love of the bricks and mortar. He is ashamed of the pride he takes in seeing this new factory completed, the workers hired, the equipment in place. But it's beautiful to him. And he knows he has done the job well despite his bitterness.

Heading for the truck, he stops to admire the stars. Back home, the stars are so much dimmer. Here, they are a canopy of light lashed down to the horizon. He looks up at the splash of the Milky Way across the heavens and wonders how he will find a way to feel clean again. But the stars only wink and dance. He finds no answers there. The staccato bark of a coyote jerks him back to earth. He climbs into the truck and heads into the night.

Eleven OUT IN THE COLD

Laura Silver's parents lived in a townhouse on one of those leafy streets in Georgetown where the red brick of the buildings seems to sing of money and power. Sam looked up at the brick facade and wondered what the evening would bring. He was wearing the sartorially safe outfit of khakis with a blue blazer. Bringing a bottle of wine into a house likely to be populated with wine connoisseurs was a high-risk strategy. Instead he carried a sleeve of freshly cut flowers.

As he mounted the steps to the townhouse, he had a strong sense of apprehension about the evening to come. He liked Laura a great deal. He even felt he knew her fairly well. After all, he had heard her recite Tennyson. But he also realized that he didn't know her well enough to know much about her parents or who would be attending tonight. A deep breath. It would be OK. Here goes. He rang the bell.

Laura's father opened the door, introduced himself and pointed him toward a bar set up in a corner of the living room. Sam was glad to see that a number of guests had already arrived. But Sam saw right away that he didn't fit in. There's a certain style in Washington that the men and women acquire. It's a look of certitude and grace, a look that says my time has come or will be here soon. It's a way of walking, of talking, of careless laughter.

Sam didn't have this style. It's a style born out of the exercise of power or influence. Sam knew that its acquisition came at a price, but he envied the other young men and women standing with their drinks looking nonchalant while he stood clutching his flowers and gracelessly modeling his blazer and khakis. To hell with them, he thought. Maybe he would recover some self-assurance by finding Laura's mother and getting himself a drink.

As he looked around, he saw Laura at the foot of the stairs. She made her way toward him. She was wearing a long black skirt and a cashmere sweater. Sam thought of Sinatra singing "The Way You Look Tonight." Why hadn't Sam ever noticed how beautiful she was? Her face had a freshness and a vitality that made the rest of the people in the room look dull and flat by comparison.

"Sam! You made it! Come meet my family." Laura took Sam's arm and a great sense of relief washed over him. He wondered if there was some way to keep her anchored to him for the rest of the evening.

Sam survived the introductions to mother and brother Andrew, guardian of the consumer and protector of the minimum daily requirements of the man on the street with his V-8-juice-filled briefcase.

"So this is the famous Sam," Laura's mother had said as he handed her the flowers. He was surprised and flattered that his reputation preceded him. It had never crossed his mind that Laura might talk about him with her parents. Laura offered Sam a glass of wine and he took it happily.

Soon everyone made their way to the dining room. The table was set for twelve, the crystal, china, and silver ablaze in the light of the chandelier. Most of the guests were friends of Andrew's from various government agencies or law firms around the city. The table came alive with witty banter and gossip about the Washington scene. Emboldened by the wine, Sam's forays into the conversation became more frequent. He was pleased to see his humor and insights being well received.

For Laura, the evening couldn't be going better. She had fretted all day over whether Sam would fit in with her family and Andrew's friends. She shouldn't have worried. Sam was doing fine. And the wine was having its way with her as well. Now that her worst anxieties had proven groundless, she was immersed in the conversation at her end of the table.

As the plates were cleared and dessert was brought out, Laura found herself savoring the evening and wondering why she had been so nervous. She looked over at Sam, chatting away with one of Andrew's friends. It was a wonderful night.

Her reverie was interrupted by her brother's voice. A brief silence had fallen over the table as the dessert plates were put down. In that silence, Andrew, who was sitting across from Sam at the midpoint of the long table, cleared his throat theatrically and fixed Sam with a glance and a smile.

"Tell me, Sam," he said in an overly loud voice. The conversations around the table stopped in anticipation of Andrew's remarks. "Laura tells me you don't believe in government regulation of corporations. She says you're a big fan of unrestrained capitalism."

Sam knew when he was being baited. And he usually liked rising to the bait. But Laura's presence on the other side of the table made him uncharacteristically cautious in responding. Laura saw Sam tilt his head quizzically. She saw him hesitate. Laura found herself hoping he would brush the comment off, make a joke, tell Andrew anything at all other than what he really felt.

"Who could like unrestrained capitalism?" asked Sam innocently. Laura began breathing again. Sam was a good guy. And a wise one not to take on her brother.

"After all," continued Sam, "under capitalism, man oppresses man. But under socialism,"—here Sam paused—"it's the other way around."

Some of the guests chuckled in appreciation, waiting to see how Andrew would respond.

"Come on, Sam, I'm serious. We're not talking socialism. Just the obligations of a corporation beyond the bottom line. Do you really believe that corporations have no other obligations beyond profit? That's some Milton Friedman thing isn't it? No one believes in that Neanderthal stuff any more."

Later that night at home, when Sam recalled the evening's events, he was able to pinpoint this moment as the one where he inwardly said to hell with it and let himself go. The linking of Milton Friedman with "Neanderthal" pushed him over the edge.

"Responsibility is a funny word," said Sam. "It conveys a sense of obligation, which in turn conveys a sense of debt, of owing something. What precisely would you have in mind when you speak of corporate responsibility?"

"You don't have to be pedantic," Andrew said. "You know what it means. It means treating your workers well. It means making products that are safe. It means treating the environment well. It means caring about the community."

"Those are lovely sentiments. But they're meaningless platitudes. Does the responsible firm never fire a worker? Always offer health insurance? Day care? Eight weeks of vacation? High wages? When profits are low or negative?"

"You're just being contrary," Andrew said. "It may be hard to define precisely, but there are clear cases when a company acts irresponsibly. How about when a shoe company puts its plants in some Asian country and exploits the workers there?"

"And how is that irresponsible?" Sam asked.

Andrew snorted in exasperation.

"I suppose you think it's responsible to pay workers 30¢ an hour," he said. Instead of looking at Sam, Andrew looked around the table for approval.

"It beats the alternative," Sam said.

"Which is?"

"Earning even less than 30¢ an hour. After the shoe company moves its factory to the United States, you can buy shoes with a clean conscience. Of course you've taken a job away from that poor unfortunate in say, Indonesia. Eventually the unemployed workers there may find another job. But it will probably pay less than 30¢ an hour."

"You're ducking the question," Andrew said. "Instead of closing the factory in Indonesia, the shoe company could instead decide to pay a living wage."

"In Indonesia, 30¢ an hour *is* a living wage. Those people aren't slaves. The shoe company doesn't have them working at gunpoint. Do you think when the announcement was made that a factory was coming and that jobs would be available, people said, no, keep it away from here? They danced in the street and lined up for the opportunity to be 'exploited.' The tragedy isn't that they earn 30¢ an hour. The tragedy is that 30¢ an hour is their best alternative. They're near subsistence because their economy is low on capital and they lack skills and education. Not because they're being exploited by multinational corporations."

"That's nice. You're here living in comfort in America. Don't you find it a little presumptuous to call 30¢ an hour a living wage?"

"Fine," Sam said, ignoring the insult. "You want higher wages for Indonesians. Who should pay for it? Consumers in the form of higher prices? Stockholders in the form of lower returns for their investment? Americans who work for the shoe company in the form of lower wages? What you really want is a welfare program for Indonesians paid for by the shoe company."

Andrew gave a brief laugh of derision. "Come on. That's a caricature."

"I don't think so," Sam responded. "You want to do good. But you ignore the fact that someone must pay for it. It's easy to do good with other people's money."

"You sound like an accountant. Productivity can go up when pay increases. Workers will take more pride in their work." Andrew said.

"You sound like a science fiction writer. When it's in a company's self-interest to pay more than the market will bear, then companies don't need cajoling or regulations to be more generous. It's in their own self-interest to do so. But to pay beyond that is no more than a welfare payment."

"But what's the harm in encouraging extra generosity and improved social performance? Everyone benefits."

"But they don't," Sam replied. "That's what makes the whole concept so pernicious. Under the guise of being good-hearted, it masks the real choices taking place. There's no free lunch. Inevitably someone must pay for the generosity you're encouraging. Often it's the very workers you claim to care so much about. According to you, the responsible corporation should provide health care benefits, worker's training, and day care. But the workers pay for these benefits in the form of lower wages or fewer job opportunities."

"Right," Andrew said sarcastically. "The benevolent corporation at work. Anything to avoid a minimal drop in profits. The sacred bottom line must be preserved. If the cost of labor goes up, just take it out of the workers' hides."

"But it's not the corporation's fault. When you make the job more attractive with better fringe benefits, more people want to work there. That's what drives down wages."

Sam could feel his engine revving toward the redline, but he couldn't help himself. His mood was affecting Andrew's as well.

"That's the most creative justification I've heard for corporate greed in a long time. You blame the workers for their own exploitation."

Laura recognized Sam's point as the same one he had made about teacher's salaries.

"What he's saying Andrew," Laura interrupted, "is that there's a supply and demand for labor. When the supply of labor increases, wages go down."

"Since when did the next Erica Baldwin learn to think like Ayn Rand?" Andrew was highly irritated to hear his sister parroting the views of this compassion-free economist across the table. "Since when are you the queen of unfettered capitalism?"

"I'm just trying to clarify the argument," Laura said, blushing. "I didn't say I agreed with it."

Andrew turned back to Sam, "You live in a fantasy world where workers and consumers are fully informed and everything adjusts smoothly."

"And in your world," Sam countered, "only *you* are fully informed. Everyone else is in need of your wisdom."

"You just can't stand the idea that your beloved marketplace can produce inequitable or disastrous outcomes. You spent too much time in grad school swallowing those theories about the marketplace and the invisible hand. Too often that hand is at the throat of the worker or the consumer. We need more benevolent corporations, guided by social policy."

"I'm not as arrogant as you are," said Sam.

The tension level in the room went up another notch. Laura found herself thinking of ways to derail the conversation. It was dangerously out-of-hand. It was one thing for her and Sam to spar over economics. But this was getting nasty. She looked over at her parents for help but each was absorbed in the argument and failed to catch her eye.

"You're wiser than the marketplace," Sam continued. "Even wiser than the workers who must live with their choices. You would treat adults like children. You would ban cigarettes if you could—"

"Of course I would."

"Again you know what's best. In the name of corporate responsibility, you applaud the corporation that gives to charity."

"Don't you? Or is charity too good-hearted for your taste? Listen to what you're saying. I would ban cigarettes. You would ban charities to make sure the poor get their character improved by poverty."

"You couldn't be more wrong, but let's stick to corporate behavior. When a corporation makes a donation to charity it can be good public relations. It can help advertise the name of the company. It can help make the community a better place to live, making it easier for the corporation to attract workers. That's fine. But if the CEO donates the corporation's money to the symphony because he likes schmoozing with musicians or to a homeless shelter because he fears political pressure and the implicit threat of regulation from people like you, then it's a different matter."

"What's wrong with that? You're just proving my point that you don't care about people. Who cares why a corporation gives? If the result is more art or a homeless shelter or a program for crack-cocaine babies, what difference does it make? My goal is to make the world a better place."

"But it's not your money." Sam was trying to control his anger and keep it out of his voice but he was losing the battle. The wine, the traded insults, and his feeling of being besieged by the silent disapproval of the other guests were all pushing him past the point of no return.

"What are you talking about?"

"The corporation's money. It's not yours. It's not yours to give to workers in the form of fringe benefits even if it did make them better off. It's not yours to give to charity even if it makes the world a better place."

"That's sophistry and nit-picking. That money came from the community. It belongs to the community. So the community should have a say in how it is spent, not just the CEO."

"You're half right," Sam countered. "It's not the CEO's to spend as he wishes. But the CEO *does* have a responsibility. To the stockholders. They've invested their money with the company. They've taken the risk. They're entitled to the return. When a CEO builds a lavish corporate headquarters as a personal indulgence it is wrong. It's just as wrong for a CEO to spend it on a pet charity. The CEO should use that money to hire better workers or modernize factories or whatever is best to ensure the long-run viability and profitability of the enterprise. That's true corporate responsibility. And in my world, the marketplace disciplines the CEO and enforces that responsibility, not some government official in Washington susceptible to political influences or an elitist social critic. You would justify your actions with the consolation that you're making the world a better place. In your mind, people don't know enough to spend their money wisely. In your mind, stockholders are a bunch of fat cats clipping coupons. They'll 'waste' the money on frivolity, on yachts and fancy cars, money that could better be spent on goods you deem to be more important. But I reject your calculus of the good."

"Are you through?"

"Andrew," Laura pleaded.

"This man is a snake," Andrew said, looking at his sister. He turned to Sam. "You're dangerous. You justify corporate greed in the name of working people. You make Ayn Rand sound like a social worker. You defend the Charles Krausses of the world and all who would make money on the backs of others. And I resent you poisoning my sister with your heartless view of the world."

Everyone at the table awaited Sam's response, anticipating another flurry of verbal serve and volley. Sam took a deep breath.

"You know nothing of my heart."

Sam turned to Laura's mother.

"Mrs. Silver. I seem to have worn out my welcome." Sam did not wait for the perfunctory denial. "Thanks for a lovely dinner." He stopped and looked over at the rest of the table. "I'm sorry to have spoiled dessert."

He looked at Laura. She was staring straight ahead and refusing to meet his gaze. Sam held his head high and made as graceful an exit as he could. The night air was cool on his face. Well, that's that, he thought. Sam headed for home, burning with shame and anger at the thought of the conversation continuing back at the dinner party. There would be laughter and mockery. He imagined Laura joining in. He couldn't blame her. He had made a mess of it.

When he got home, he paced around the apartment, furious at himself for what he had done. How could he have let himself be provoked? What was he thinking? Thirty years old and he couldn't manage to control his emotions. He lay on the couch, staring at the ceiling and rehashed the arguments of the evening thinking of how he could have expressed himself better. A waste of time. He should have just laughed the whole thing off when Andrew started up with him. But he knew in his heart that he couldn't stay silent on something he felt so strongly about.

His eye caught the pile of books on the coffee table. There was the anthology he had bought just yesterday, a collection of English poetry that included Tennyson's "Ulysses." The sight of it turned his stomach. Who did he think he was, angling for the affection of a woman like Laura? He reached over and flung it across the room with a vicious backhand.

The pages spilled out of the cheap paperback on impact. The sight of a destroyed book drained away his anger. He sat down and put his hands over his face. A few deep breaths. He turned off the lights and put on Sinatra's "In the Wee Small Hours." He lay there in the dark, listening to the title cut. He thought of Laura earlier in the evening, standing at the foot of the stairs, her smile taking his fear away. How could he have been such a fool?

When the doorbell rang Sam had fallen half-asleep and only caught the echo of its last ring, bringing him to the surface. Reflexively he looked at the clock. It was 1:00 A.M. His adrenaline surged at the thought of Laura, coming to see him and salve his wounds, telling him it was all right. He raced to the door. He flung it open in expectation, but there was no one there. At his feet lay an envelope. In the distance, he could hear the echo of running footsteps. Who had brought him mail at 1:00 in the morning?

Back inside, he turned the envelope over but other than his name on the front, it had no markings. Sam had given an exam that day. The envelope was probably from a student seeking special dispensation for missing the test.

But Sam didn't remember anyone missing the exam. He opened the envelope. Inside was a note. "Hope these help. A friend." Along with the note were a set of credit card receipts and a confidential memo on government stationery. The name on the receipts and the memo sent a jolt through Sam that made him put the papers down. The receipts had been signed by a prominent Senator. A Senator whose view of the world was very different from Sam's. A Senator who was in the headlines every day as a key figure in a Senate probe. And a Senator Sam refrained from mentioning in class because the Senator's daughter was one of his students.

Sam picked up the memo again and read it carefully. He immediately saw the connection between the receipts and the memo. Now all he had to do was figure out what to do about it.

Twelve THE CORNERED BEAST

"Of course this is merely a hearing. We are here to share ideas with one another and to explore a variety of, well, avenues that need exploring. Questions have been raised, and these questions, after all, must be delved into and examined. Again, I want to emphasize the informality of these proceedings."

Senator Lash is known for his rambling introductions with as many meanderings as the rivers of his home state of Oregon. He has been in the Senate for what seems forever.

"We are here to look at some of the crucial, the critical, aspects of our economic system. We have decided to focus on HealthNet, well, because, well, for a variety of reasons. We on the Committee are grateful for the cooperation of the Office of Corporate Responsibility, otherwise known as the OCR or 'Okra.'"

Senator Lash looks up from his notes and beams paternally at Erica Baldwin, who is sitting near the front of the gallery.

"Okra plays a critical role in our free-market system," Lash continues. "They are the watchdog of the system, barking when something goes amiss. Nothing is more dangerous than unfettered greed running rampant through our streets and shopping malls, from Main Street to Wall Street."

Erica Baldwin pretends to be looking through some papers. She finds Lash unbearable and though she agrees with the substance of his remarks, she knows that most of his statements are for the camera and do not represent any deeply held principles. She looks up to hear Charles Krauss being introduced as the first witness.

She hates him. She hates him for what he does and that he feels no guilt for his actions. She has to be careful. Letting her emotions and ego get involved is dangerous.

The investigation of HealthNet has begun to take on a life of its own. These hearings are the beginning of the process. Soon, if things go as she has planned, events will start to build. People with stories to tell will start coming forward. She still hasn't figured out what the documents she received in the mail could mean.

Senator Lash asks the first question.

"Mr. Krauss. I would like to open these hearings with a general question. What do you believe to be the responsibility of a corporation in the twenty-first century?"

Krauss pauses before replying. He looks over his shoulder to where members of the HealthNet legal staff are sitting and flashes a quick grin. They are already on edge, worried about what he might say. Krauss's grin makes them even more uncomfortable, even more uneasy than before.

"Corporate responsibility in the twenty-first century," Krauss begins, almost musing to himself. "Very impressive sound to it. Let's see—the corporation in the twenty-first century has many responsibilities, to its community, to society at large, and to mankind. Grand enough? Should I add the universe as well? Truth be told, I have one and only one responsibility"—here Krauss pauses—"and that is to make money."

A collective gasp goes up from the gallery. Krauss again looks over at his lawyers. He gets a perverse sort of satisfaction from seeing them so miserable. There is only one thing he dislikes more than laws—lawyers. They thwart so many of his plans. The least he can do is make them squirm from time to time, even if they are on his own staff.

Senator Cashman of California is recognized. He has been the catalyst for the formation of the OCR. And although Lash is the chairman of the committee, everyone recognizes Cashman as its driving force.

"Surely Mr. Krauss, you have some responsibility to your employees and their communities. Your employees make your products. Their communities create the quality of life that makes it possible for your workers to live well there."

"I pay their salaries, don't I? Too damn much at times. My board of directors thought such generosity might help me avoid a circus like the one I'm performing in here. Clearly to no avail."

One of the HealthNet lawyers groans audibly.

"Well I am glad we contribute something to the common good, Mr. Krauss," continues Senator Cashman. "Let us move to some more specific areas. Does HealthNet have production facilities in the People's Republic of China?"

"You know we do."

"And what is the average wage of the workers in those plants?"

"That is proprietary information."

"And does HealthNet have production facilities in Mexico?"

"They have just come on-line."

"And what will be the average wage of the workers in those plants?"

"Alas. Proprietary again." Krauss beams at the panel and shrugs.

"Perhaps you do not wish to share the details, Mr. Krauss." The speaker now is Senator Carmen from New York. "But it is public knowledge that many of your workers outside the United States earn less than a dollar per hour. Do you think it fair to pay such low wages?"

"Fair? I don't know what fair means," he says innocently. Hoots of derision come from the gallery. The chairman silences them. "I receive no complaints from my workers," Krauss continues.

"They're probably afraid to speak up, Mr. Krauss," the Senator continued. "But we have accounts of numerous manufacturing accidents in addition to the privations of low wages."

"I wouldn't trust second-hand accounts, Senator. I would be happy to arrange a tour of any HealthNet facility at your convenience."

Erica stops listening after a while. This is standard stuff. Her mind wanders over the possibilities for the future of the Health-Net investigation. Eventually, the Senators tire of pounding on Krauss with such little impact. They turn to the next witness. Erica looks up to see him take his place in front of the microphones. The man's name is George Sutherland. He looks familiar and then Erica remembers. He and his family have been on the cover of Time magazine as symbols of the new insecure economic landscape. That story had helped build public demand for hearings into HealthNet.

Sutherland takes his place at the table and adjusts the microphone. He does not have Krauss's imperial bearing. He is also visibly nervous. Senator Perkins of Ohio tries to put him at ease.

"It is a pleasure to have George Sutherland, a citizen of the fine state of Ohio here to speak before our committee. Welcome to Washington, Mr. Sutherland."

"Thank you, Senator Perkins."

"You are from Matalon, are you not?"

"Yes I am, sir."

"It's a fine town. A fine town. It is not unlike many small towns throughout Ohio and our great nation. Full of good people, good families. People eager to work and work hard." Senator

Perkins isn't talking to George Sutherland anymore. He is addressing the chamber and giving George a chance to find his composure and relax. After another minute of extolling the virtues of small-town America, Senator Perkins turns his attention back to the man at the microphone.

"I understand you have brought some photographs with you."

"I have."

Senator Perkins gestures to an aide who scurries forward and sets up three easels to the left of George Sutherland. Each easel holds a corkboard. George hands the aide a large manila envelope. She opens it, takes the pictures out and tacks them to the corkboard. They are the haunting faces of the Mexican children whose parents work in the HealthNet factory in Mexico.

It is a marvelous tableau. At the center is George Sutherland, about as American a man as you can find. The fact that he is ill at ease in his best suit and new haircut increases his dignity. On one side of him are the photographs of the children in rags standing in front of their miserable shacks. Clothes flap in the background. A goat nuzzles the legs of one child. On the other side of George Sutherland is the well-fed, angry face of Charles Krauss. This triptych will make a riveting picture on the front page of America's newspapers.

"Can you tell us about these photographs, Mr. Sutherland?"

"Oh sure. When I worked in Mexico I'd see these kids three or four times a week. They live with their families in those shacks you can see in the background."

"Have you been in those"—Senator Perkins searches for the right word—"dwellings?"

"Many times. One of my supervisors lives in that one right there." Here, George gets up from his seat and points out the structure.

"Are you telling me"—the speaker now is Senator Cashman— "that a supervisor earns a wage that puts him in the hovel we're looking at?"

"I'm afraid so."

"And how much would that wage be?"

"I don't think it would be right to say, given Mr. Krauss's testimony earlier. But I think you get the idea that it's not a great deal of money."

"What were you doing in Mexico, Mr. Sutherland?"

"I was working for HealthNet."

"I take it you are no longer employed by HealthNet."

"I'm not employed by anyone. I'm looking for work."

"Have you received any payment to testify today?"

"Absolutely not!" George stops. "Sorry, sir," he continues, in a calmer voice. "I'm here on my own nickel. It seemed like the right thing to do."

"It is and you are to be commended for it. Are these pictures yours?"

"I purchased them from a friend who took them."

"They are very striking."

Rob Blankenship, sitting in the gallery with the HealthNet group, recognizes the settings for the pictures. He tries to show the concern he thinks appropriate for a caring person seeing such extreme poverty for the first time. And of course he knows who took the pictures. But George has bought his silence. Blankenship will say nothing about Alice to his boss and in return, George will not tell the press of Blankenship's ugly little attempt to suppress the photographs in the first place. George was able to convince Blankenship that it would be bad publicity if it were known that Blankenship tried to destroy the pictures. Nor will it be good for Blankenship's relationship with Mr. Krauss for it to be known that his attempt was unsuccessful. Blankenship had come around to George's point of view very quickly.

Now Senator Cashman asks George to talk about Matalon and the impact the closing of the factory has had on the town. Erica is enjoying herself immensely. She loves the pictures. They will do as much for her cause as the cover story in *Time*. There will be more leads from this publicity. More sordid episodes from HealthNet's impact on people's lives. She feels her pager vibrate against her side. She looks down. It's a local number she recognizes.

She leaves her seat in the gallery, ducks into the hallway and snaps open her cell phone. She returns the call.

"This is Erica Baldwin returning Dr. Levine's call. Yes, I'll hold." She taps her foot nervously, waiting for him to come on the line. "David, this is Erica Baldwin returning your page."

Erica listens intently for two minutes. She nods from time to time.

"Thank you, David. You've made my day."

Which is really saying something, Erica thinks as she makes her way back to her seat. She wouldn't have thought it possible to top George Sutherland's testimony. She forces herself not to smile as she returns to her seat in the hearing room.

Thirteen THE RULES OF THE GAME

By the middle of May, with the end of the school year rapidly approaching, Laura's desk was a rolling landscape of papers and piles of books. She had a free period and some grading to do. Rather than face her desk, Laura found a classroom in the basement where she could have some quiet and spread out her work.

Over a month had passed since the dinner party at her parents' house. She hadn't spoken to Sam other than a curt hello or two in the hall. He had sent her flowers with a note that said, "Sorry about the other night. I hate Nike." She hadn't responded. She sometimes saw him eating lunch by himself in the school's courtyard. The time she had read the Tennyson poem to him seemed so long ago.

The classroom Laura sat in was part of a larger classroom split in two by a room divider. Renovations in the rest of the building had put this room into use. While Laura was grading her papers, a class was going on in the other half of the room. Laura, sitting at the teacher's desk, was far from the divider. But she could hear voices raised in argument. Curious and eager to procrastinate, she went over to the divider. She recognized Sam's voice. It was his elective class, "The World of Economics." She leaned closer to hear what was going on.

"I know it's not fair, but I'll state the rules again," she could hear Sam say patiently. The rules? Laura figured Sam's class was a bit unusual. She was ready for anything short of human sacrifice. But she was still surprised to hear Sam's class playing some kind of game.

"Here are the rules," Sam continued. "You are a dictator. You can pass one law while you are dictator. One law and one law only. And it has to be a *law*, not merely a good intention. You cannot simply decree that people love one another or that disease come to an end or that nobody get hurt in car accidents. You must defend your choice mindful of the laws of nature and the laws of economics. Now who would like to begin?"

"I would pass a law requiring all students to graduate from high school," a girl's voice suggested.

"Why?" Sam asked.

"High school drop-outs cause a lot of problems. They commit crimes. Then they have trouble finding jobs and they end up on welfare."

"So everyone would have to stay in school. Do you think it would be hard to monitor compliance?" Sam asked.

"Not really."

"Would you take attendance everyday? And what would you do with people who were absent?"

There was a silence as the student thought about possible punishments.

"Would you punish them after one violation?" Sam asked. "Two? Three?"

"Three seems fair," came the response.

"I don't know," said Sam. "I think you'd still have a problem with kids leaving once the attendance got taken. But let's suppose everyone complies with the law. What are you going to do about the kids who don't want to be there and ruin class for the others? Of course what you'd really like is a law that forced all students to stay interested in their classes. But that is against the rules. But perhaps you can think of something that would encourage student interest. How about someone else?"

"I would eliminate all welfare payments entirely."

Laura was surprised to recognize Amy's voice, a student in her senior poetry class. Amy's father was a Senator. A Senator who was a long-time defender of expanded welfare programs. How was Sam going to deal with her suggestion?

"What are you going to do about the children of mothers on welfare? Let them starve?" Sam asked.

Amy hesitated before answering. "We could have a temporary program, just for helping the kids."

"How temporary? Six months? A year? How would you make sure the kids got the money and not the parents?"

Sam let Amy think for a moment. He must have been pacing.

"We could have special restaurants where only kids could eat. That way we could make sure the kids didn't starve while the parents look for work," Amy replied.

"That's creative. And what would you do if at the end of the program the parent still didn't have a job? Leave them to starve?"

"Tough. The parents would have an incentive to find a job if they knew their kids' food was going to run out."

"Good point," Sam conceded. "But for a threat to be effective you have to be willing to carry it out. Would you be comfortable letting those kids go hungry?"

"Private charity would take care of them."

"Maybe. There's a theory in economics which says that private charities could never raise as much money as government programs raise via taxes."

"There is?" Amy asked.

Laura was equally surprised. She wouldn't have expected Sam to bring it up.

"Yep," Sam continued. "Stay after class and we can talk about it. In the meanwhile, you might want to think about how you would feel if private charity had trouble filling the gap. Who else has a proposal for the perfect law?"

The students kept proposing ideas and Sam kept poking holes in them. After a while, the other students joined Sam in coming up with unforeseen complications. Laura was surprised to hear Sam attack every proposal, even ones she thought he would find appealing. She was also impressed with the liveliness of the conversation.

It was an intriguing game. It forced you to identify what you thought to be the biggest social problem and then come up with the best way to fix it. It was amazing how differently the students thought about the problems facing the country and how differently they thought about the best way to fix them. One wanted stiffer penalties for drug use. Another wanted to legalize drugs. But no matter what was proposed, there was something wrong with every policy. Laura supposed that the point of the game was to understand the challenge of designing good policy.

To her surprise, Laura soon found herself thinking of Sam instead of the world's best public policy. He seemed to be a very good teacher and a fair one. A clamor on the other side of the wall brought her back to the classroom.

"All right, all right."

It was Sam.

"You want to know my law. Fair enough. The one thing that I think would most transform America and make it a better place. But even though I believe it to be the best law, I would not pass it even if I were dictator for a day. Your job is to figure out why."

The class grew quiet.

"If I could pass one law," Sam continued, "and one law only, it would be—"

Sam stopped for what Laura assumed to be dramatic effect.

"It would be," Sam began again, "to ban television."

Sam's suggestion was met with total silence. Laura was surprised as well. She was expecting a ban on regulation, getting rid of the minimum wage, or something related to economics. A ban on television?

"Watching television is a total waste of time. It's the secret addiction. It saps everything from us that is human. It turns us into zombies, flitting from channel to channel to escape reality."

Someone in the class must have snickered for Sam responded.

"You laugh. How many of you watch at least one hour of television a night? At least two? Three? Do you think you could go cold turkey? Do you think your life would be richer if you went cold turkey?"

Laura could imagine Sam through the wall, pacing and waving his arms to make his point. She started to smile. She had forgotten about the stack of papers on the desk.

"Ban television and children begin to explore the world rather than sitting stupefied in front of the sterile box in the corner. Ban television and families talk to each other over dinner. Ban television and people begin reading again. Ban television and a person can learn to sit and think, a lost art in the television age."

"But some television shows are good," a student interrupted.

"Aha!" Sam cried. "Just like every policy we have discussed, there's a cost. But I'm confident that the benefits far outweigh the costs. There are probably a few good shows. But the sewage far outweighs the spring water. Violence, sleaziness—"

Some members of the class giggled at the old-fashioned nature of this tirade. Laura smiled at the thought of Sam, the nineteenth-century man, offended by the prurience of television.

"You laugh," Sam said. "But it takes a toll on human decency. You're thinking it's no big deal. You're right. It is no big deal. And that's the tragedy. After watching MTV your attitude toward women is cheapened. If you watch enough murders on television, then real murders become unfortunate annoyances rather than tragedies of immeasurable proportion."

Sam stopped to catch his breath.

"I'm a little passionate on this topic. Maybe a little *too* passionate. But I speak from experience. I'm a recovering addict. When I realized how many nights I lost, hand on the remote, surfing the cable channels, I sprung into action. First I put the television in the least comfortable room in my apartment. Then I dropped cable. Finally I sold my set. I'm free! And I'll tell you something. I read more books, do more volunteering, and spend more time talking to my friends and my family than ever before. But I don't fool myself. I remain an addict. When I'm in a hotel, I can't help myself. I flip on the set and flip out. So I have no illusions about my ability to handle the problem. And now we've got the Internet. Another great temptation to avoid real life."

Laura grinned at Sam's honest self-assessment. What a strange man he was.

"Now," Sam continued. "I believe that television is hazardous to your brain. But you know what? If I were dictator for a day, I still wouldn't ban it if I could. Do you know why not?"

There was a tumult of answers but Sam quieted the class.

"I'd like to let you guess, but it's late, and there's one more game I want to play. It will help you understand why even if I were dictator, I wouldn't ban television."

Laura had totally forgotten about her grading. Not wanting to miss a word, she pressed her ear against the divider.

"This game isn't my invention. It comes from an extraordinary book by Robert Nozick called *Anarchy, State, and Utopia*. Has anybody read it?" Sam paused. "Of course none of you has read it. You're too busy watching trashy TV."

The class laughed in response to Sam's sarcasm.

"In *Anarchy, State, and Utopia*," Sam continued, "Nozick describes a peculiar machine. Let us call our version a Dream Machine. Once you have programmed it correctly and you are hooked up to its sensors and electrodes, you experience any life you can possibly imagine—the ultimate game of virtual reality. Any dream will come true. While you are on the machine you can be President of the United States or the greatest rock star of all time. You can climb Everest, cure cancer, win an Oscar, make a billion dollars a year. And here is the magic of the Dream Machine. Unlike the dreams of slumber, these dreams will feel totally real. You will be lying on a table, hooked up to the Dream Machine, but in your consciousness you will be surfing flawlessly in Hawaii, singing the most popular song of all time, winning the NBA championship for the tenth time in a row, and it will all be as vivid as the feel of the pencil in your hand and the sound of my voice. How many of you would like to take the Dream Machine out for a spin?"

Laura imagined every hand going up in the other room. Her mind began to conjure up fantasies she would indulge if given the opportunity.

"Of course you would," Sam continued. "But there's one detail that I neglected to mention. This imaginary life that you get to experience while on the Dream Machine must replace your actual life. You will never wake up. You enter the room today as the teenager you are. You win the Masters, the Nobel Peace prize, surpass the popularity of the Beatles, then you grow old and die. It can be a painless death, preceded by a glorious old age full of parades and honors. But after they unhook the last electrode, your brain will cease functioning and they put you in the ground. While you're on the machine, the river of time will appear to flow at the same speed that it does now, out here in the real world. But in fact, your entire time on the machine will be less than five minutes. Then they will cart you off and bring in the next"—Sam paused—"customer. Still interested?" Sam asked cheerfully.

Laura felt a chill go through her. There was silence on the other side of the wall. Finally Sam filled it.

"I didn't think so. Why not?"

"It's not real," someone called out.

"I know," Sam said. "But you won't know that it's not real. It will feel real."

"But it's fake," a student said. "While you're on the machine, you will have cured cancer, but people outside of the machine will still be dying from it."

"That's true," Sam said. "But why would you care? For me the answer is that life on the Dream Machine is no life at all. Not only because it's not real. But also because the Dream Machine strips life of everything that makes life worth living. The striving, the seeking, and the finding."

Laura exulted to hear him using the ending of "Ulysses."

"And the failing," Sam continued. "Where's the magic of the 'finding' if you can never fail? If I offered you a billion dollars a year for the rest of your life, no questions asked, and the only string attached is that every year you must spend every dollar, would you take it? If you did, would you be happy?"

"Of course you'd be happy," a student said. Laura imagined heads nodding around the room. She could think of worse experiences.

"For a while, you'd be deliriously happy," Sam continued. "Imagine the first day. Lobster and caviar for breakfast, lunch in Paris after a brisk trip on the Concorde with a few hundred close personal friends, then dinner in New York in the Presidential Suite at the Plaza. The second day, lobster and caviar for breakfast again, maybe a new restaurant in Paris for lunch or perhaps for a change of pace, you'd have the best chef in the world fly to New York to cook you lunch. Maybe you'd have the New York Philharmonic play background music to entertain the luncheon guests you're hosting at the Guggenheim Museum that you've rented for the day. Then later that night, courtside seats sitting with Spike Lee at the Knicks game. OK, so maybe you wouldn't choose the Philharmonic, but you get the idea. It's amazing for a day. Extraordinary for a week. But for a year? Ten years?"

"I'd like to try," said a student. The class's laughter came rippling through the wall.

"I know. It sounds appealing. But after ten years of caviar for breakfast, caviar tastes like corn flakes. Let me tell you a story."

The room went quiet. Sam must have been gathering his thoughts.

"A man dies," Sam said, "and finds himself on the bank of the most beautiful trout stream in the world. The sky is a burning blue and a perfectly balanced fly rod rests in his hand. Before him lies the water, a perfect trout stream, a mix of rapids and slow pockets of water. All his life he had wanted to find more time to fish. He realizes that he's in heaven. He looks upstream, a swirl, a fish has risen for an insect! He makes an exquisite cast to the exact spot. In an instant, the water explodes as an enormous fish surges to the surface, chunks of water flung from its sides as it strikes. The flash of power and color causes the man to gasp in awe. After a brief struggle he lands the fish. It must weigh twelve pounds! And the colors are so vivid! He releases the fish, and turns back to the water. Again, a fish rises for an insect. Again, he makes a perfect cast. Again, he lands the fish, another beauty. It's a miracle. The man falls to his knees in gratitude to God. But as the day wears on, fish after fish after fish breaking to the surface in answer to his efforts, a thought begins to flutter at the edge of his consciousness. He decides to try a deliberately poor cast. Still, the fish rises and he brings it in. He starts yelling and thrashing the water to spook the fish. It does not matter. Every cast yields a fish. And he knows that he is not in heaven after all."

A student asked, "What's it have to do with banning television?"

"Because banning television is against the rules of the game. Not the rules of our game in here, but my rules of the game for the good life. The good life is real. It's full of ups and downs. Success and failure. Coming up out of the valleys makes the view from the peaks exhilarating. Catching a fish on every cast isn't heaven. Having a billion dollars is boring. Banning television doesn't bring us closer to the good life—it doesn't really transform the world. It papers over what is wrong and makes you think you've solved the problem, a dangerous delusion. Why do you think the stuff on television is so degrading? Because people like it. Why do people watch for four hours a night and fall asleep at the clicker? Because their lives are empty. Banning television doesn't change any of that. And even if it could, what right do I have to make those dysfunctional families talk more often? What right do I have to force parents to actually spend time with their kids? And even if I had that right, why would you think that using that right and treating adults like children and taking away the candy of television is the way to transform the world? I'm proud of not having a television. It's a triumph, albeit a minor one, over my baser nature. Isn't that what life is all about? Coming to know yourself and finding a way to do what is right? What's the good of having the government do it for you through a law that reduces your choices? That's not life. Any more than if we changed the rules of the game and considered a world where the government could end anger or jealousy or greed or lust or violence. Life in that world would be no life at all."

Sam stopped. The room was silent.

"Time's up. See you guys tomorrow."

Laura wasn't surprised that she was interested in Sam's oration. What surprised her was that she cared enough to tell him. She wanted to skip her next class. She wanted to see him, to talk to him. Laura finally understood something about him. He was a sheep in wolf's clothing. She resolved to find him later that afternoon in the teacher's lounge and apologize for not responding to the flowers he had sent.

As Laura passed the door to Sam's part of the divided classroom, she saw a crowd of students around Sam. Off to the side was Amy, the Senator's daughter. She appeared to be waiting for Sam. She was tall and blond, star of the girl's volleyball team, editor of the school paper, and Stanford-bound next year. That girl, no, that woman, could cause Sam a lot of trouble. Perhaps she already had.

Not for the first time, Laura wondered what Sam could possibly have done to merit dismissal. From what she had heard over the last forty-five minutes and from the buzz of students challenging him after class, Laura was sure that Sam was a teacher who made his students think. Surely, the quality of his teaching was not the problem.

Fourteen S E R I O U S   N U M B E R S

"I have some important news."

Erica Baldwin is talking at the regular Monday morning meeting of the OCR. She has been quiet, listening to Marshall Jackson, the lead staffer on the HealthNet investigation update everyone on the progress of the HealthNet investigation. She is not prone to dramatics. But her announcement and the way she makes it grabs everyone's attention.

"This package came here about two weeks ago," she says, holding up a 9- by 12-inch manila envelope. She pulls a sheaf of papers out of the envelope. "It came through our P.O. box for anonymous tips. I showed these to some of you when they came in. We knew they had something to do with HealthNet—an employee sent them to us. But we didn't know what they were. No identifying marks. Just some long columns of numbers and letters. I've stared at them for two weeks waiting for some clue to jump out at me. I now know what they are."

Erica pauses and takes a sip of coffee.

"These are the data from a set of clinical trials required by the FDA for any new pharmaceutical," Erica continues.

"How do you know?" someone asks.

"On a hunch, I sent them over to Levine at the FDA—we've talked to him before on clinical trials. He's been there for years. He recognized them right away and paged me on Friday, while I was at the hearings on Capitol Hill. There's what's called an International Code of Harmonization, or ICH. All trial results have to conform, so they all look pretty much the same."

"So what do they tell us?" Marshall Jackson asks.

"That's where we need some luck. Levine tells me that we only have a partial set of results. Here, take a look."

Erica hands around copies of some of the pages.

"The far left column is a subject number. They go up by ones. The first page we have starts with number 1583. That means we're missing the first 1,582 results plus all of the preceding material. The next sixty pages have the same layout. What we have is probably part of the appendix from a report. Unfortunately, we're missing the summary charts at the end."

"So what do these pages tell us?" Marshall Jackson says.

"We don't know," Erica answers. "The presumption is that if someone wanted to destroy these records, then they're hiding something. But what?"

"But there's not even a company name on these. How do we know they're from HealthNet?" a staffer asked.

"We don't. Levine will check that out for us. Some of the numbers at the top identify the company. Every test has to be registered with the FDA."

"So if we only have a piece of a piece of the report, have we learned anything?" Marshall Jackson asks.

"I think so," Erica says, a smile spreading across her face. She leans back in her chair with contentment. "I think I've figured it out."

∞

"You're new here."

It is a statement, but the woman behind the desk takes it as a question.

"Yeah. Heather quit. I'm filling in until they find someone permanent."

Howard Cantrell tries to think of something else to say, but he is out of conversation. He retreats awkwardly to the small sitting area just outside of Charles Krauss's office. There is a black leather couch, a leather armchair and a glass coffee table of irregular shape. Cantrell picks up the annual report lying on the table and tries to find it of interest. He fails.

Cantrell is staring off into the distance when the secretary smiles at him and tells him that Mr. Krauss can see him. He would rather read the annual report for a few more hours, but it's not an option. He enter Krauss's office and nervously sits down across from Krauss's desk. The last time he appeared before Krauss was to warn him of problems with the new prostate drug. Now he's here at Krauss's bidding.

"This report is much better." Krauss holds up a ringed binder. "I knew you could work things out."

Cantrell says nothing in response to Krauss's remark. He just wants to leave.

"I'm not expecting any more problems," Krauss continues. "Or any surprises. No more bad news, right?"

"No."

"I took care of that—material—you sent me," Krauss says. "I told you there was no need to worry about it. These results are more like it. How's your conscience?"

"I don't have one. That's the right answer, isn't it?" It is the closest Cantrell comes to defiance.

"More or less. At least you had enough sense to give me that heads-up. But your hands are clean. I told you I'd take care of it and I did."

The Director of Research responds with only a glassy stare. He has an urge to say "no comment" or to simply start scream-ing. He is grateful for his self-control.

With a gesture, Krauss dismisses him.

∞

It is almost eight o'clock when Erica Baldwin unlocks the door of her Georgetown apartment. She has stayed late and taken her time getting home. She lays her briefcase down on the dining room table. Her dining room is small but serviceable. She rarely entertains. Inevitably, the dining room table becomes her over-flow desk, the place she gets her work done when the desk in her home office becomes unmanageable. She slowly gathers up all of the memos and documents she has been working on from nights past. Tonight, instead of putting a placemat down for a quick dinner, she takes her laptop out of its case and sets it humming in the clear space she has made.

Before she sets to work, she goes over to the CD player and puts on Paul Simon's *Hearts and Bones*. She takes the manila envelope out of her briefcase and pulls out the sheaf of papers. She takes a deep breath. Her body swaying to the rhythms of the music, she begins entering number after number into the spreadsheet.

Fifteen SWEET CHARITY

Sam Gordon sat placidly on a bench in Dupont Circle in late May, oblivious to the young couples strolling to dinner, the joggers and the street people talking to themselves, oblivious to everything other than the poetry he was trying to understand in a book with a missing cover, his brow furrowed in concentration.

The rumble of a bus broke the spell. Sam looked down at his watch—a little before 7:00. Laura had invited him to dinner at her apartment at 7:30. He shoved the book into the front pocket of his backpack and headed up Connecticut Avenue.

Sam had been surprised when Laura approached him the other day after class. He was even more surprised when she invited him to her place for dinner. She made no mention of a change of heart or why she hadn't responded to his efforts to apologize. She merely joked that her brother was not invited and told him that her roommates would be out for the night. It would just be the two of them.

Laura was renting a house with three college friends, a few blocks short of the zoo on Connecticut. Sam found it easily enough. It was just before seven-thirty. He took a deep breath and rang the bell.

Laura opened the door. She was wearing jeans and a T-shirt. Sam was surprised at how glad he was to see her standing there, smiling at him.

"Hello, Sam. Come on in."

"Hello, Laura. Sorry I'm late." He was still breathing heavily from the walk. "Here," he said, reaching into his backpack. "I brought you something."

Laura looked down at the CD and giggled.

"I know," Sam said. "It's a ridiculous title. And when you think of Frank Sinatra, you probably think of your parents. Or your grandparents. But trust me. 'Songs for Swingin' Lovers' is the American popular song at its best."

"Thanks, Sam." She smiled at him. "Come into the kitchen. I'm about to start dinner."

Sam followed Laura down the hall.

"Would you like a beer?" Laura asked when they reached the kitchen. "We're having Chinese."

Sam took the offered bottle of Tsing Tao and sat on a barstool at the island in the middle of the room. The beer was ice-cold. On an empty stomach, it was delicious.

"Can I help?" he asked.

"I'll let you know."

"Laura," Sam began. "I'm sorry about that night at your parents. I—"

"Forget it. Water under the bridge. Clean slate." Laura took a canister of rice down from the pantry shelf. "Are you hungry?"

"Starved," Sam admitted.

Laura measured two cups of rice into a saucepan, added some water and set the flame on high.

"I have my own apology," Laura said. "I was very upset after that night at my parents. I had no intention of ever talking to you again. But that was childish. I should have responded to your flowers. I—"

"It's OK. Clean slate, remember?"

"OK."

Laura turned the rice down, covered it, and set a timer for fifteen minutes. She took two chicken breasts from the refrigerator and began slicing the meat into strips. When the chicken was cut up, she put it in a bowl, sprinkled it with cornstarch, white wine and black pepper, swirled the mixture with a chopstick and put it aside.

"Do you have any brothers or sisters, Sam?"

"One sister, in Houston. She works for the great friend of the working people, ExxonMobil."

"There's a polluter in Houston by the same name. Is that the one you mean?" Laura asked, winking.

"I don't know. The ExxonMobil I know goes to immense expense to find crude oil around the world, pull it out of the ground, refine it, and sell it to people so they can get to work and the beach and visit their friends and family. They do spill some oil once in a while. No free lunch, you know."

"So I've heard. What's she do there?"

"She's an engineer."

"Younger or older?"

"Older."

"So your sister's an engineer in the business world. You seem to love business, too. Why aren't you out there looking for twenty-dollar bills or helping someone else find them?"

"I hear that getting and spending, you lay waste your powers."

"Who told you that!"

"It's in a poetry book I'm reading. An anthology of British poets."

Laura stopped in the middle of taking a sip from her beer and looked at Sam with surprise.

"I'm trying to civilize myself," he continued. "Opera is next. Then I was thinking of moving on to the big stuff. Modern art. A subscription to the *New York Times*. Then who knows, maybe *The New Yorker*. I can dream, can't I? Actually one of your students asked me about your Wordsworth quote. But I *am* reading the anthology. And if you want to know the truth, I decided a long time ago to give up the big corporate bucks for the privilege of being an underpaid high school teacher."

"Funny." Laura paused from her work and wiped her hands on her apron. "Can you peel garlic?"

"I suppose. How hard can it be?"

"Hard enough if you don't know the trick. Watch." Laura showed Sam how to use the side of a knife blade to crush the garlic cloves and make them easier to peel. Sam set to work. Laura began mincing a scallion. Sam pushed the cloves over to Laura and watched with fascination as she minced the garlic in seconds, holding the point of a butcher knife to the cutting board with one hand and rocking it back and forth across the garlic with the other. Taking a cleaver, she hacked up a broccoli head into flowerets and then picked up four carrots. After peeling them, she methodically worked the knife to create one translucent orange coin after another. Once the carrots were sliced, Laura went to the pantry and pulled out various bottles and jars. The timer rang and Laura turned the rice off and let it sit with the cover on.

"What's this?" Sam asked, peering at a chrome machine full of strange knobs and handles sitting on the counter. "I'm guessing it has something to do with coffee."

"It's called a La Pavoni. It makes the best espresso outside of Italy. Isn't it beautiful?"

"It's so beautiful that a tea drinker would think of buying one just to admire it from a distance."

"Not if he knew the price. I took last year off and went to Israel and Italy. My parents said they'd buy me one if I came home," she said smiling. "It worked."

"I'm glad."

Laura put a big blackened wok on the stove and set the flame to high. She stood looking at Sam, hands on hips. "So here I am, sitting in an empty classroom the other day, catching up on my lesson plans, and I hear this guy in the classroom next door, through the partition. I can tell it's a good class because the conversation is alive. A lot of back and forth. You know what I mean? People are so excited, they're fighting to get their point across. I edge closer to the partition. I'm getting drawn in to the discussion myself. And then the teacher, his voice sounds awfully familiar—but I'm having trouble placing it—and he tells this story about a fisherman."

"Ahhhhh."

"I won't bore you with it. But it's a beautiful story. It's the kind of story that someone in that room might remember for a long time. I figure it's a philosophy class. But it's not Stanley, the philosophy teacher. The voice is all wrong. Then the class ends with this story about money not being that important. Must be Ellen, who teaches psychology. But it's definitely a man's voice. Did I mention that? So when the class is over I went out into the hall. You'll never guess whose class it was."

"So tell me."

Laura pretended not to pay attention. She ignored Sam's request and poured some oil into the wok. She waited for the oil to get hot.

"Sam Gordon," she said finally. "Can you believe it? It was Sam Gordon's class. Truth is, I'm not really surprised. But here's what I can't figure out. At the beginning of the class, I could have sworn I heard the teacher defend the welfare state. But how could

Sam Gordon, the lord of laissez-faire, the deserter of the down-trodden, lecture his students on the virtues of the welfare state? And then at the end of the lecture, the same guy, who is supposed to be an economist, tells the students that money isn't important. I can't figure this guy out. Who is this Sam Gordon, I ask myself."

Sam smiled and sipped his beer. "Sam Gordon is a man who eats a lot of pasta with spaghetti sauce out of a jar. Tonight, he is a very lucky man."

"No doubt. But do you actually like welfare programs?"

"You're not going to stop cooking if I give the wrong answer, are you?"

"Probably not."

"Actually, I am not a big fan of government welfare."

"That's it," Laura said in mock disgust, throwing her hands into the air. "I'm stopping."

"No," Sam wailed in mock horror. "I'll burn my Adam Smith tie. I'll read Dickens every night. I'll sit at the FDR memorial and weep for the golden years of the New Deal."

"All right. Let me do some work with the wok and you can explain yourself over dinner."

When the oil in the wok was hot, Laura stir-fried the meat then removed it from the wok. Then she let the oil heat up again. She tossed in the garlic and some dried hot peppers. The garlic sizzled in the hot oil and the pungent aroma filled the room. Then Laura added the broccoli and the carrots. After a few minutes, she added rice vinegar, white wine, soy sauce, hot pepper flakes and finally, toward the end, so it wouldn't get dried out, the chicken. All the while, Sam marveled at her dexterity with the spatula as she flipped and turned the contents of the wok. It wasn't quite the equal of the recitation of "Ulysses" for Sam, but it was close.

Sam and Laura moved into the dining room. Laura dimmed the lights, lit two candles and served up the food. Sam was ravenous. He fought off an urge to plunge in with his chopsticks. He waited for her to begin.

"Cheers," Laura said, raising her beer.

"Cheers," Sam answered.

They drank. "Hang on," Laura said, jumping up. "Be right back."

She went to the living room. Sinatra began singing "You Make Me Feel So Young."

"You don't know what a treat this is for me," Sam said when Laura had sat down again.

"The food or the music?"

"The company. The food and music are just the spice."

They ate, talking of school and the challenges of dealing with adolescents. Laura filled Sam's bowl again, then refilled her own.

"So tell me," she said. "What's wrong with welfare programs?"

Sam looked into her eyes. She was smiling and waiting for him to speak. He saw the same open face, full of wonder and life that he had seen across the table that evening at the coffee shop. He had an urge to say nothing, to change the subject and ask her about Chinese food, or opera or the Italian countryside. He realized that for the first time in a long time, he actually cared about what someone thought of him. He hesitated. Was there a way to say how he felt without sounding like an ogre? What a strange sensation, worrying about how he came across!

"You go first," he ventured. A defensive strategy seemed more likely to succeed. "Tell me *your* perspective on welfare programs."

"My perspective is simple. I see people starving and I want to give them food. I see homeless people, I want them to have shelter. I see people hurting and I want to see them healed."

"My perspective is more complex. You know me—I like seeing people starve to death. Did I ever tell you about the time I was chatting with someone on the subway and she called me—was it malevolent?"

"I think it was satanic."

"That's it. But being against free health care for the indigent doesn't mean being against health care for the indigent. Being against food stamps doesn't mean being in favor of hunger."

"Sounds awfully similar."

"I'm against *government* solutions to these problems. But I don't believe in the virtue of selfishness. Or that the crucible of capitalism heals all wounds—or that it raises everybody's standard of living, nonstop at every moment. I want to fight poverty without the help of the government."

"If the food stamp program were cancelled, do you think a lot of people with the lifestyles of the rich and famous are going to suddenly grow a conscience, drive into the bad part of town, and bring people home for dinner?"

"Not many would. But some would give money to charities that fed the poor and some would give money to charities that would try to do more than feed the hungry. Ever hear of Maimonides?"

"No."

"Jewish philosopher, thirteenth century—he was the high point of Hebrew school for me. Maimonides understood that when charity is given, there are two sides to the transaction, the giver and the receiver. He was worried about both. He wanted the giver to have a pure heart and the receiver to have dignity. And Maimonides said that according to Jewish law, the highest level of charity is when the giver makes a gift or a loan or gives some other form of help that lets the receiver become self-sufficient."

"Give a man a fish and he eats for one night, teach him to fish and he never goes hungry."

"Right. Maimonides was also very concerned with anonymity as a way of maintaining dignity and purity of heart. The lowest level of charity is given with a grudging heart where both giver and receiver know the other's identity. I think Maimonides felt that it was demeaning to the receiver to know who he was beholden to, but he also felt it was unhealthy for the giver to know who he was supporting. I learn three things from Maimonides. First, independence should be the goal. Second, the dignity of the receiver must not be forgotten. And third, and we often neglect this, the soul of the giver counts too. Although it's better to give than not to give at all, the ideal is to give gladly rather than grudgingly. The ideal is to give before you're asked. The ideal is to give out of compassion rather than for the egotism of having someone depend on you. That's why I think Maimonides cared about anonymity of both giver *and* receiver. So while it's nice to take a beggar home for dinner, the best thing you can do is help him become independent. I wouldn't expect private charities to replicate the food stamp program. I'd hope they'd find a way to help people help themselves."

"But isn't money what they need to help themselves? You're always talking about how people know what's best for themselves. Why not give them money and let them figure out what they need? Don't they know better than someone running a charity?"

"It seems obvious that if you don't have enough money, money is the solution. But I think Maimonides would say that the solution is whatever it takes to make the person independent. If it's drunkenness, he might need sobriety more than money. If it's bad luck, then he does need money, but only for a limited time. If he's poor because he has few skills, help him educate himself. Consider two imaginary charities. The first one is called, say, Acme Charities. Their motto is 'One size fits all.' The second is called Custom Charities. Their motto is 'Every soul is special.' At Acme Charities, if you have low income, they don't ask you why. They just give you money. Over at Custom Charities, everybody's treated differently. They get to know you. They try to tailor their help to the individual. Which charity would you donate to?"

"Custom Charities, of course," Laura answered.

"But you can't, because nothing like it exists. Acme Charities is out there, though. Its real name is the Department of Health and Human Services. Government-run welfare programs are remarkably inflexible. They probably have to be for legal reasons. There's no way a government official can dole out money or food stamps on a case-by-case basis. As a result, Acme is best at reducing suffering. It's lousy at creating independence."

"So why do you give money to Fast Eddie?"

"Because I'm only giving him a dollar. There's no way to give a dollar's worth of help that will let him stand on his own feet. When I give a dollar I'm only trying to dent his despair. It's an act of compassion to let him buy a drink. It's little more than a gesture. But private charities in a world without government assistance would do more than just hand out food. And I'd be willing to give a lot more than a dollar to help change Fast Eddie's life if there were a charity that knew how to help him. A charity that could combine my money with that of others to make a real difference."

"But if you want to change Eddie's life in the most dramatic way, wouldn't cash do the trick? If you're going to help a motorcycle rider with his medical expenses, why not let him ride without a helmet, you told me. Well, the lesson seems to be the same here. If you're going to help Fast Eddie, why does the amount matter? Help him on his terms. Give him money. If he wants to stay a drunk, let him. And if he wants to change his lifestyle, he can do that too if he chooses."

"I believe in being generous in the face of suffering, but I've got my limits. I'm not willing to guarantee a comfortable lifestyle for every poor person regardless of why they're poor. I want a different kind of help for people depending on their situation. I'm willing to give money with no strings attached to solace someone for a while who's down on his luck. The challenge is to avoid turning the safety net into a hammock. The government is good at creating a hammock. To produce a chance at true self-reliance, we should try Custom Charities."

"So why doesn't Custom Charities exist if it's such a good idea?"

"For Custom Charities to raise any money, it's going to have to convince you to pay twice. You've already paid your taxes that go to pay for food stamps and rent subsidy programs and Medicaid. Are you going to make an additional contribution to help the poor on top of that? The government basically has a monopoly. If the government stopped fighting poverty, then Custom Charities would have a chance to flourish. And it wouldn't be a monolithic, single agency. There would be a whole bunch of private charities in competition which means more choice for donors and more choice for the poor. It also means more innovation. Some charities might simply give money to the poor, but they might struggle to raise money from donors. Some would attach strings to their aid and they might struggle to attract clients. The best charities would be those who did the best job satisfying the demands of both their donors and their clients. There would be a lot more variety than we see now under the government system. Some private charities might offer mentors. Some would offer temporary assistance. Who knows what innovations they might come up with?"

"I worry about whether that system will raise enough money. I think most people are selfish and taxation is the only way to get any money out of them for the poor. I'm not going to stand by and wait for some rich guy to open his checkbook. Aren't you his shill, providing an argument for his opposition to paying taxes to help the lazy poor?"

"Whoa," Sam said. "I'm not a shill for anybody."

"Maybe you're a pawn then. Aren't you serving the rich guy who opposes welfare programs just because he hates paying for them? And doesn't it make you suspicious of the truth of your views when they're the same views as someone who is purely selfish?"

"I've never thought about it. It's a disconcerting thought."

"Suffer with it for a moment while I clear the table."

"I'll help. It will give me time to recover."

Sam's mouth was on fire. His palate was not prepared for the hot pepper onslaught. He was glad to see her scoop raspberry sorbet into two bowls and head into the living room to continue talking. Laura turned the Sinatra down a bit.

"You might be right," Sam said, once they had settled into the couch. "I am, unwittingly, the ally of the selfish. That may explain why people sometimes treat me like I'm heartless. They assume that if I'm against forcing people to give through the tax system, then I'm against helping the poor. But I'm *not* like your selfish rich guy. I'm *in favor* of helping the poor. I don't want people to go hungry. I just don't think it's right to force people, even selfish people, to give. If we want to make the world a better place, I much prefer to work on creating compassion in selfish people rather than using the Internal Revenue Service to force them to give. Worse, forced giving destroys the satisfaction that altruistic people get from doing the right thing and giving voluntarily. It deadens the soul. We human beings have this overwhelming desire to keep what is ours. To overcome that desire and share with others is an essential part of our humanity. A world of private charity allows us to express that feeling. A world where the government takes care of the poor takes the compassion out of life."

"That's a nice idea, Sam. But if most people aren't compassionate, are you willing to wait until they're transformed and the poor suffer? You told Amy that if you eliminate government pro-grams, private charities won't raise as much money as the gov-ernment spends now."

"Amy." Sam rolled his eyes. "She's more Catholic than the Pope."

Laura laughed to hear Sam compare himself to the Pope.

"Sometimes she's too free-market even for my taste," Sam continued, "at least in the way she expresses it. I take the oppo-site view with her to try to get her to think. That's when you heard me defending welfare."

Sam paused for a moment, hearing Sinatra's effortless ren-dition of "I've Got You Under My Skin." He was singing "Don't you know little fool, you never can win." And for a moment, Sam wondered why he was arguing about poor people with Laura, try-ing to make the case that he was a decent human being after all.

"Sam?"

"Sorry. Where were we?"

"I wanted to know why you told Amy that private charity wouldn't raise as much money for the poor as the tax system."

"You heard right. If we got rid of welfare there probably *would* be less money going to the poor. Even if most people are altruistic."

"Why's that?"

"People know that others are giving. This encourages some people to give less than they would otherwise give and others to give none at all. The total amount is likely to be much smaller than in a tax system where you can force people to give. So what's good about tax-based help for the poor is that it raises a lot of money. What's bad is that it leads to a monopoly."

"Couldn't we raise the money through the tax system and let private charities decide how to spend it?"

"That might be an improvement over the current system. You lose the virtue of people giving voluntarily. You create a political challenge of picking which charities get the money. I'd rather try an all-private system even if it raises less money."

"It seems to me it could be more than just much smaller. It could be zero. People already give money to the charities they like. If the government stops collecting taxes and giving it to the poor where will people find the money to give to new charities that you think will spring up?"

"If the government gets out of the charity business, the current recipients of food stamps and every other program are going to have a tough time. Caring people will want to help them. Look at education. The public school system in the inner cities is an embarrassment. A total failure. To give kids in the inner city a chance, people have started scholarship funds to let poor kids have the chance to have the chance to attend a private school."

"You mean vouchers?"

"Think of these funds as private vouchers—they use private money, not tax dollars. As a result, they get designed without political pressure or concern over church and state issues. For example, they typically cover maybe half of the tuition at a private school."

"Why only half?"

"Making the parents pay for at least half of the tuition creates a commitment on part of the parents. I used to think public schools were mediocre because they didn't have to compete for customers. Now I think that's only part of the problem. The other part is that they're free—there's no out-of-pocket charge to the parents. When people have to pay directly for something, they treat it as precious. If vouchers get funded out of tax dollars, there will always be political pressure to raise the amount of the voucher. You asked about rich guys growing a conscience. Well, two really rich guys, Ted Forstmann and John Walton, pledged $100,000,000 to one of these funds. And lots of less wealthy people, including me by the way, have made donations to that fund and others like it. People are so upset with the quality of the public schools in the inner city that they're willing to give away large sums of money on top of what they already pay in taxes to subsidize the public schools. I think Maimonides would really like these scholarship funds. What better way to fight poverty than to improve the education of poor kids?"

"That's a nice example, but I don't have your faith in the ingenuity of private charities."

"I have none in the ingenuity of bureaucrats. The current system is the road to hell. Between the welfare system and the public schools, we've destroyed a generation of children. We've got to try something different."

"Haven't we tried your solution already? It's called 'the past' and it was a failure. Isn't that why the government had to get involved during the Great Depression?"

"That's the myth, but state and local governments were already involved before the Great Depression. There was also a thriving network of private charities that helped the poor. What changed with the Great Depression was an enormous increase in the involvement of the *federal* government giving away dramatically larger sums of money. Just like Acme Charity, the government drove the private charities out of business. Private charities in the 1930s couldn't raise any money. They effectively went bankrupt."

"Maybe people just couldn't afford to support them. Maybe the Depression hit the rich too hard."

"Maybe. But a private solution has a better chance of working now than it did in 1930. We're a lot wealthier. There's over $100 billion donated to private charity in the United States today."

"So why isn't it making more of a difference? You've been telling me that there's no chance for innovation. But $100 billion should be enough money to come up with some creative solutions."

"Very little of that money goes to the poor. Instead it goes to religion, health, the arts, and education."

"Don't religious groups help the poor?"

"Some. Most of the religious money goes to religious institutions that spend it on their buildings and their religious activities. Imagine a church using church funds to help single mothers. Donors would want to know why they should give money to a cause already covered by their tax money. In today's world, private charities that *do* help the poor focus on people who slip through the cracks in the government programs. Street people. People with no addresses or who don't have the mental wherewithal to wait in line, fill out forms, or deal with a government official. But get rid of public help for the poor, and private charities that fight poverty in creative ways will have a chance to thrive in the same way those private scholarship funds have the potential to make a difference. But you want to know the truth?"

"I always want to know the truth, Sam."

"I could be wrong. It might not work. Maybe private charities will be no better than the government at giving people money in ways that avoid the destructiveness of dependency. And maybe they'll make things worse because they can't raise enough money."

"This is a first. Maybe I should tape this. Do I detect some gray there, some ambiguity in the Sam Gordon worldview? A hint of uncertainty, perhaps?"

"You bet. Enjoy it. But there are no perfect solutions to the poverty problem. We can dent despair but it takes more than money to end it. The only solution is to let time pass and let capitalism do its work."

"But capitalism created the poverty we're trying to fix. Even you have to admit that capitalism can't solve the distribution of income."

"You're right if your goal is egalitarianism. For that you need a totalitarian government willing to create a Gulag Archipelago for people who fail to cooperate. And even then, communism in the Soviet Union created a terrible, unbridgeable gap between the haves and the have-nots. The party elite lived like kings and the man in the street waited years for a tiny apartment. Ironically, it's capitalism that has destroyed poverty with unparalleled success."

"How can you say that when ten miles from here there are people living in horrible conditions?"

"That's because you're looking at the present, just one point in time. You have to look across the generations. Think about my grandfather. He had to quit school when he was twelve to help keep his family going. That was the end of his formal education. His life was never easy. When the Depression came, the business he had started went broke. He had to swallow his pride. He and his wife and kids moved in with a cousin for two years. Then he became a peddler, selling bedspreads and lamps and linoleum out of the back of his car to the poor people of Memphis, Tennessee. He did that for the rest of his life. The days were long, the money was mediocre, and the work didn't exactly challenge his mental abilities. How many ways are there to describe the virtues of a bedspread? At night he read Shakespeare and quarreled with a world that made him get in that car every day and fight the heat in the summer, the cold in the winter, the customers who didn't pay and worst of all the resentment that he was meant for better things and would never have them."

"That's an American tragedy."

"I don't think my grandfather thinks so."

"Is he still alive?"

"No, he died years ago. I was speaking figuratively. There were millions of Americans at the turn of the century just like my grandfather. Some were in the mines. Some were in the textile mills. Others were on the newly built assembly lines. Those men, and they were mostly men, worked ten or twelve hours every day, six days a week, sometimes seven."

"The system chewed them up and spit them out."

"That's the way it appears. But what should we have done for those men? What was the alternative to those hardships? We could have given them money to ease the economic burden. But that money would have had to come from somewhere. We could have legislated shorter hours and better working conditions, but that would have meant lower wages, fewer jobs, and less productivity. If we had gone to the extreme and shielded those men and their families from economic hardship, we would have eliminated the suffering. We also would have eliminated the incredible growth that transformed America over the last century. Because my grandfather scraped and saved, his son—my father—was able to go to college and escape the grind. His grandson, yours truly, has it even better. And do you know why? Because the system refused to put my grandfather and others like him in an economic cocoon. It took a toll, but it also paid dividends. My grandfather's sacrifices and those of his generation created what we have today. You can't have one without the other. While my grandfather was alive, he looked like a victim of the system. But the passage of time gives his life a different meaning."

"That doesn't change the fact that your grandfather had a miserable life."

"He fed his family and gave his children a chance to succeed. His life had moments of despair. But was there an alternative that would have removed the misery without removing the life we have today? I don't think so. I think my grandfather ended up with a good deal. Fortunately he lived long enough to see his son and grandson succeed, educationally and economically, in a way that he could never have done for himself. I like to think he loved my dad and me and the rest of his grandchildren enough to make that deal a good one for him."

"You're the only guy I know who can make misery sound inspiring."

"Capitalism involves struggle, but it has an invisible heart beating at its core that transforms people's lives. If you give it the chance. Look at the full picture and you get a very different perspective."

"I don't know. You told me you're not a shill for the selfish. But aren't you arguing for leaving the poor alone because suffering is ennobling?"

"I don't want to romanticize the day-to-day existence of my grandfather and argue it was a bowl of cherries. It wasn't. I just think the tough times he went through spurred him and my father to try harder. But I'm not blind to the difference between suffering and total misery. There's a big difference between a beggar in Calcutta and the poor in America. It may be impossible for the beggar in Calcutta to rise above his position. But it is possible for the poor person in America to rise. We have seen it done generation after generation here. And we know the secret in America: hard work coupled with decent education."

"Capitalism may work in the long run. But isn't the short-run problem of today something we have to deal with? Doesn't it create too much inequality?"

"I don't know what that means."

"Sure you do. The rich are getting richer and the poor are getting poorer."

"That's what you hear."

"Do you think it's true?"

"I don't know. The numbers people use to measure inequality have all kinds of problems. There's a lot of room for ax-grinding there. Here's what I do know. If you think inequality is bad in and of itself, the best thing you can do is improve the education system for the children of the poor. That's the best way to make a difference that's real and lasting. That's why I give money to those private scholarship funds."

"And what about those who don't get the education or who don't have the work ethic? What about racism? Not everybody can make it. Are you willing to stand by and do nothing?"

Laura was surprised to see Sam jump up from the couch, pacing, the words coming in bunches.

"Do nothing? I don't want people to starve. I don't want people to go without medical care. I've told you I believe in charity. If there weren't a government-run food stamp program, I'd give money to private charities that made sure people didn't starve. If there weren't a government-run health program, Medicaid, I'd give money to help people get medical care who couldn't afford it. Wouldn't you?"

"Sure, I would. I'm just not sure there are enough people like us."

"I think there'd be millions. And the result would be a system where people have an incentive to train themselves to deal with economic insecurity. A system where people have more of a chance to stand on their own two feet. I believe in softening misery but not while creating a cocoon of dependency. Maybe that's not possible, but that should be the goal. Life is about striving. Life is about achievement. Life is about failing and getting up and trying again."

Sam stopped abruptly. "What was the last line of that Ulysses poem?" he asked.

"To strive, to seek, to find, and not to yield."

"Yes. That's what being a complete human being is all about."

Laura shook her head in amazement. "You're an idealist, aren't you?"

"I don't know. But here's something I do know, with no shades of gray. You're a great cook."

It was late. Sam needed to get home. Both of them needed to sleep. Over Laura's protests, Sam did the dishes. He praised the food again and thanked her for dinner. Then he collected his backpack and standing in the doorway, turned back toward Laura.

"Are you busy, Thursday night?" he asked. "Can I take you to dinner?"

"I've got plans, Sam. Sorry," she said, sensing his disappointment. She hesitated for a moment. "Hey, why don't you come. I'm having some friends over. I've got to warn you—the evening may test your patience. But come."

"Is it a dinner party? You've probably realized that dinner parties are not my strong suit."

"Food will be served, but it's not the main event. It's a surprise. Don't worry, it'll be fun."

Sam wondered what she could possibly have in mind. An evening of discussing Jane Austen? Karl Marx? There were a lot of topics that would test his patience.

"Just tell me the time. I'll rustle up some Valium or Prozac."

Laura laughed. "Come at 8:30." Laura paused. "Can I ask *you* something, Sam?"

"Sure, anything." Sam saw Laura's face soften. He could tell she was going to ask him something more intimate than his views on poverty or his availability for dinner Thursday night.

"Have you been fired?"

The question took Sam by surprise. He wasn't sure what to say.

"I'm sorry," Laura said, "I know it's none of my business. I've just heard these rumors at school."

"I've been fired," Sam said finally, in a quiet voice. "For now, anyway. I have a right to a hearing to appeal the decision. It's been scheduled. But to be honest, I haven't decided whether to go through with it or to cancel it."

"Sam—"

"Don't worry," he said, moving to the doorway, "it's not about sex or drugs or anything remotely exciting. I'm not a monster. I think you'll be on my side." He looked at her for an early sign of whether she might be convinced. "I'll tell you the whole story when it's over. Promise."

"I'm sure it will turn out OK," she said, in as hopeful a voice as she could manage.

She was wrong, Sam thought, but looking into her eyes he saw the trust and comfort that he needed. On an impulse, he took her into his arms and held her. Her face turned upward to his. Her kiss was softer than he could ever have imagined.

Sixteen THE NUMBERS ARE HEARD

It is almost midnight. Erica Baldwin is still at the dining room table. The computer is still humming there. Wielding a pair of chopsticks, she picks out a piece of chicken from the white take-out carton. She takes a deep breath and gets up from the table. Everything rides on what comes next. She is in no hurry to roll the dice. So she pads into the kitchen and makes a cup of tea.

Then she returns to the table and takes a deep breath. She pauses. Now. She pounds out a sequence of keys then leans back and waits. The numbers dance as the spreadsheet responds to her commands.

Then she pounds out another sequence of keys and waits again. Her brow wrinkles in puzzlement. She pounds out the same sequence of keys. She waits. Come on, come on, she mutters to the numbers as they wriggle across the screen. When the same numbers come up again, she throws herself back into the chair in surprise and frustration. She gets up and begins to pace back and forth. Then she slows down, hesitates, then stops. She smiles and closes her eyes in delight and laughs out loud. It's too late to call Marshall Jackson. She'll tell him in the morning.

∞

"You have reached the office of David Levine at the Food and Drug Administration. I can't come to the phone right now. Please leave your message at the sound of the beep and I will return your call at my earliest convenience."

"Dr. Levine, this is Erica Baldwin. It's a few minutes after 8:00, Tuesday morning. I was hoping to catch you before your day got started. I'll try you later."

Erica hangs up the phone and makes a primitive effort at straightening up her desk. As on most mornings, this means little more than taking the papers on her desk and putting them into taller and straighter piles. As her staff begins to arrive for the work of the day, she tells them to be prepared for a meeting at 9:00.

There is an excitement in the air as the meeting begins. Erica sits in her usual chair, arranging the papers in her lap, absorbed in them. Everyone else speaks in muted tones, eager for the meeting to begin. Finally, Erica looks up.

"Last night I took these home." Erica holds up a sheaf of papers filled with numbers. "These are the numbers we were sent, the pharmaceutical data. I started playing with them last night based on what Levine over at FDA was able to tell me."

Erica pauses and passes out some sheets of paper around the room.

"This is a typical page," she continues. "The first column is the subject number. The second column is a letter, either an A or a B. Levine says that's a treatment group. So the As might be getting the drug while the Bs get a placebo. Then there are two columns of numbers. The first column is typically the 'before' while the second is the 'after.'"

"Meaning?" someone asks.

"It depends. I spoke to a friend of mine last night, a stockbroker on Wall Street. He told me that HealthNet is rumored to have a number of drugs in clinical trials right now that are anticancer agents. So say this is a drug designed to fight a tumor. Then the first column is the size of the tumor in millimeters before the treatment, while the second column is the size after treatment. Normally, there's a table at the end of the appendix that details the efficacy of the drug. It takes the mean size of the tumor before and after to see if the drug shrinks the tumor at all. Then there is a statistical test to see if the difference is large enough to be attributable to the drug or whether it might have occurred by chance."

"But we don't have the table," Marshall Jackson says.

"No, we don't," Erica says. "But we have something that is almost good enough. We have enough data here in these sixty pages to figure out whether the drug works or not. As long as someone's patient enough to enter all of the A and B data into a spreadsheet to sort it out."

A chorus of voices interrupts Erica, all wanting to know what she knows.

"Hang on," she continues. "Last night, I entered all the data that we have here. It's about two thousand observations. About a thousand As and a thousand Bs. That's more than enough for statistical reliability. I did the Bs first. No effect. The mean of the first column, the 'before,' is the same as the mean of the second column, the measurement 'after.'"

"Exactly the same?" someone asks.

"No, not exactly. That would be virtually impossible. But the means are identical out to three decimal places. The difference between the 'before' and 'after' measurement is statistically insignificant, meaning that the odds are overwhelming that the difference is due to chance, the variation you would expect to find when any two groups are compared."

"How do you know all this stuff?" Marshall Jackson asks, laughing.

"When you work on enough discrimination cases as I did when I was younger, you inevitably learn some statistics. Anyway, I figured that B was the placebo. Then I looked at the results of the subjects of the A treatment. They're presumably getting the drug, not the placebo. I checked the means and compared them. It didn't make any sense. I figured I'd hit the wrong set of keys or something or transposed the commands. So I did it again. Same result. The 'after' number was bigger than the 'before.' That means on average that the drug is causing the tumor to get *bigger*. Well, you can see why I was surprised. But then I thought about where these numbers came from. They came with a note saying someone wants these destroyed. If you found out that the drug you were working on causes a tumor to grow, you might be tempted to shred the evidence. Particularly in the culture of a company like HealthNet."

"You're suggesting that HealthNet is still working on a drug they know is dangerous. It doesn't make any sense," a staffer asks.

"Not to me or you. But take a look at what HealthNet's stock has done lately. HealthNet's stock is up fifteen percent over the last month. A friend of mine on Wall Street tells me it's because of optimism about drugs they have in clinical trials. If this drug turns out to be a loser and never comes to market, HealthNet's stock will drop dramatically. That puts a lot of pressure on some-one to do something about it. Pressure to shred records and fal-sify new ones."

"You might be right, but it's just a theory so far," Marshall Jackson says.

"You're right. But this afternoon, I'll call Dr. Levine again. He'll be able to confirm that this drug is indeed a HealthNet drug. He may even have already received test results on file that have been faked to contradict these or make the treatment look successful. Either way, we'll be able to destroy HealthNet and probably Krauss along with it."

The room explodes with excited conversation. All the years of effort, of legwork, of waiting for a breakthrough may be over.

Finally, the room quiets down. People return to their desks. Erica goes to her phone and tries Levine again. She is thrilled to hear him pick up the phone.

"Dr. David Levine here."

"David. This is Erica Baldwin. I just wanted to talk to you in more detail about those test results we discussed yesterday, the clinical trials."

"Yes?" His tone is unsure, hesitant.

"I sent you some documents we had received with little identification other than—"

"I remember the documents." The cautiousness remains in Levine's voice. What is going on? Erica has known this man for almost ten years.

"Were you able to verify the company code as HealthNet's?"

"Yes, it appears to be."

"That's wonderful news. Listen, I've analyzed the numbers. There's something remarkable there, hard to believe really. I'll bring the numbers by and show you what I've done. But what I need to know now is your availability."

"For what?"

"To testify on the Hill about these documents. I think we have the smoking gun as they say. But I'd like your help."

"I don't think that will be possible."

Erica is surprised at this response. But she pushes on.

"No, no. I know you can't talk about the formal results of the HealthNet tests until they are complete. I just need you to testify about the results I sent you, the ones we received anonymously. The ones I'll show you. I would want you to identify what they represent and to talk in the most general terms about their significance."

"I'm afraid that will not be possible, either." There is a flatness in Levine's voice, a weariness, that is more alarming than if he were speaking with hostility. This is David Levine. Surely he can testify about the general scientific issues surrounding tests of pharmaceutical efficacy.

"David," she blurts out, "is there something wrong?"

"Oh no," he says quietly. "I just don't want to be in the middle of something that is unseemly. For all I know, those documents may be a forgery. Perhaps a rival has planted them with you. When you know more about their source, let me know."

"But, David—"

The line is dead. Erica's mind whirls with the possibilities. Of course David Levine is right. The documents could be a forgery. But there is more in his voice than just caution. She has the feeling that even if she could confirm the source of the documents he will not be testifying. This alone is unimportant. There are plenty of others, of lesser stature perhaps, but sufficiently knowledgeable who could speak to the issue. But what is alarming is the tone in Levine's voice, the change in her relationship with him.

Someone has spoken to him. That is the only reasonable explanation for Levine's sudden cautiousness. Someone from HealthNet has spoken to him, dangled a carrot in front of him, or brandished a stick. Or maybe a Senator has threatened to reduce his lab's funding. A Senator who is in Krauss's pocket. Maybe he has done the dirty work for Krauss. Dropped a hint. Or maybe it's less subtle than a hint. Maybe someone has made it clear to David Levine that his whole lab is under a microscope. There is to be no testifying by anyone in the FDA on matters related to anonymous documents or the whole enterprise will come under scrutiny.

But that means that someone at HealthNet knows about the missing documents. And knows enough about them to know where they have ended up. That means someone in Levine's office has notified HealthNet. Whoever leaked those documents from HealthNet is in danger and needs to be warned.

Erica reaches for the phone. She starts to dial Marshall Jackson for help in figuring out a strategy for uncovering the source of the documents. But she stops, lays the phone gently on its cradle.

What if the mole is not in Levine's office but in her own? That's impossible, Erica thinks. But she knows better. Nothing is impossible. As Director of the OCR she has seen how greed and the hunger for money produces disloyalty and worse, even in the best of human beings. Nothing would surprise her. Even a leak from her own staff. Even a leak by her protégé, Marshall Jackson. Unlikely, yes. Impossible, no. She thinks back to his behavior at the meeting. He seemed to be his usual self. He made that remark wondering where she got her knowledge of statistics. Surely he was only teasing her, not challenging her. And the other times when he raised questions. He was just playing the devil's advocate. Devil's advocate. A frightening thought. She must keep her own counsel. She will have to find the source of those documents and fast. Someone's life may be in danger. Is there any way to track down the source and send a message of warning?

But Erica has no way of tracking down her source. That is the beauty and the danger of anonymous tips. She has no way of knowing that at this very instant, Heather Hathaway is riding her bike along the canal path that runs through Georgetown and the Virginia countryside.

∞

Heather Hathaway is free. Free of HealthNet and free of worries. She hasn't even decided when she will look for her next job. The path is a great workout. This is her third time along the trail this week. The countryside is green and fresh compared to the city. It is a good place for dreaming about whatever will come next in her life.

The path is peaceful along this stretch of the canal. There are no houses or buildings. Just a few farms in the distance. The road is empty now, but if Heather looks, she can see a shape on the horizon, a car heading toward her. The air is so clean and a light breeze lifts her long blond hair behind her. Maybe she should stay in the Washington area. So many opportunities.

A red-winged blackbird lights on a fence post just across the canal. The car comes on. It is not going particularly fast. It doesn't have to. There is nowhere for Heather to hide and her mind is elsewhere, on the Virginia countryside and on her dreams. The car swerves off the road onto the path. At the last moment, Heather sees the blur of metal coming at her, but it is too late.

Seventeen SWIMMING WITH THE TIDE

In Sam's nightmare, he was back in college, taking an English class. He did have his pants on; he had not slept through an exam. But it was still a nightmare. In his dream, Sam was taking a class on the novels of Ayn Rand and Charles Dickens. He was making a presentation to the class on why capitalism was good for the poor. Every time he made a point, one of his classmates would interrupt him and accuse him of being heartless. He was a monster, a beast, a shill for the selfish. Sam lost his temper. He railed at his classmates and cursed them. Finally, in exasperation, he looked over at the teacher for help. To his horror, the teacher was Laura. She refused to look at him. She only shook her head slowly and made notes in an enormous grade book as he continued to speak.

Sam awoke with a start. Morning. It was only a dream, but it filled him with foreboding about his invitation to Laura's place tonight. He wondered what she had in store for him. He could use some advice and encouragement. It was early, but his sister Ellen would be awake already, even in Houston.

"Ellen? It's Sam," he said softly. "Did I wake you?"

"No. I'm downstairs with the kids making breakfast. What's up?"

"Do you remember that English teacher I told you about the last time we talked?"

"Sure. The one you argue with."

"That's the one. I think I'm making some progress with her—"

"What, she's reading Milton Friedman instead of John Milton?"

"No, I meant progress on the romantic front. She still thinks you save the world by fiddling with it here and there instead of letting it blossom unmolested. But I think she might actually like me a bit."

"How long have you been going out?"

"I have no idea. I'm not sure we're going out now. We run into each at school and we argue. Sometimes we have dinner together. We argue some more."

"Sounds delightful."

"I like it, actually. And I think she does too. There's less arguing lately—now it's more of a conversation. A dialogue, I think they call it. It's hard for me to recognize the concept after a lifetime of talking mainly to myself. But hey—I gave her a good-night kiss the other night."

"So what's the problem? Sounds like things are going fine."

"They are, with her. But I don't do so well with her friends and family. I've already yelled at them once. I'm invited tonight to some party or something she's planning and I'm afraid I'm going to lose it again."

"You probably will. Hang on a sec."

Sam listened as Ellen policed what sounded like a food fight or at least a skirmish between his five-year-old nephew and three-year-old niece.

"Sorry about that," Ellen said, when things were quiet again. "Where were we?"

"You were telling me how I'm likely to lose my temper. I'll be thirty-one years old in a couple of months. I think it's time to start growing up and stop yelling at people who don't agree with me. How do *you* manage it?"

Ellen laughed.

"I don't." she said. "It's an illusion. I'm an engineer. I hang out with a lot of other engineers. The ones I know don't talk politics much."

"I doubt tonight's just for Laura's engineer friends. Got any advice for me?"

"One thing I've learned in the business world is that while passion is valued, anger or agitation is not. You want to win friends and influence people, don't you?"

"I do."

"So the next time you feel your thermostat rising, think of the impact on your listeners. They're not going to be impressed by how worked up you are. It's not going to make them take your ideas seriously. It makes them think there's something wrong with you. And they're probably right."

"Thanks for the vote of confidence."

"Don't you think there's something wrong with you?" Ellen teased.

"Probably. It comes from a lifetime of political incorrectness and coping with the smugness of the opposition."

"Instead of feeling sorry for yourself, revel in it. Remember, 'Only a dead fish swims with the tide.' Enjoy fighting the current. Don't get angry. You'll live longer. And who knows? Maybe you'll get the girl."

"Thanks. So how are your two angels doing?"

"Max and Rebecca? They're perfect. As always. At least in my eyes."

Sam marveled at his good fortune to have such an even-keeled big sister to lean on when he needed her.

"Now there's an idea," Ellen continued. "Why don't you come babysit for—I don't know—maybe a few years? There's nothing like a pair of toddlers to help you practice self-control."

"I think I'll take it a step at a time. See if Max will talk to his uncle."

All day, Sam thought about keeping his passion under control and channeling it into joy rather than anger. It helped to focus on the practical notion that his ideas would have more

impact if expressed in calm maturity. Fat chance of that happening, he thought, but worth trying, whatever comes along later.

Once again, Sam made his way to Laura's apartment on Connecticut Avenue. This time the place was filled with six of Laura's
friends and roommates. They all had attended Yale with her.
They milled around the living room, eating and drinking. Laura
introduced Sam around. He smiled. He chatted. He ate. He
drank. He was actually having a good time. Where was the part
that would test his patience? Maybe he was wrong to worry about
losing his cool. Maybe someone was going to read *Finnegans
Wake* aloud for four or five hours followed by an exam. That would
test his patience, but at least he could survive it without insulting
anyone.

Then someone yelled, "It's almost nine!" Everyone scurried
around and sat down in front of the TV in the living room. So a
television show was to be the centerpiece of the evening. Sam
stifled a laugh. He could handle an hour or two of television.
Laura must have overreacted to his oration in class the other day
about the evils of television.

The room grew quiet. Sam was worry-free. He usually found
television relaxing. All he had to do was sit still and keep his
mouth shut.

It turned out to be harder than he thought. At the first break
for a commercial Laura explained that because Sam had no television, he was woefully uninformed about the previous episodes
in the show they were watching. The other guests gave Sam a
quick summary of the plot. Michael Douglas was playing one of
his standard bad guys from the business world. Intense, heartless, selfish, the usual. Once the show got under way again, it only

got worse. Why was popular culture's view of business so unrelentingly vicious? He understood that it would be hard to keep viewers interested in a drama on Wal-Mart's low prices or the great customer service at Southwest Airlines. But why did every business leader on television or in the movies have to always gouge the customer, cheat on his wife, and stop at nothing to keep profits high?

The other guests were eager to hear what an economist thought of the business issues in the show. Sam tried to speak in generalities and stay away from the real economics. Inside he was seething. He thought of his sister's advice. Keep calm. Keep calm. Desperate, he wracked his brain for a strategy, a way to maintain his composure in front of his antagonists. Then he had a flash of insight. *Pretend you're one of them.* Dead-pan, he talked about the greed of the businessman, the vulnerability of the customer, and the need for government oversight.

When the show was over, the guests turned to Sam for a final analysis. Sam kept up his facade. He said that Michael Douglas had done a great job. His character's philosophy was typical of the business world: Win at any cost. As for the scrappy government officials who had finally brought Douglas to justice, well, the world needed more people like that. Such oversight was necessary for capitalism to succeed, he explained. Otherwise, it would collapse from its own inner contradictions. Laura's friends seemed to like the new, improved Sam. After all, they had never known the original version. Fortunately, no one realized he was kidding. No one laughed or reacted with hostility to his analysis. They just nodded in agreement at almost everything he said.

As the guests left, and the roommates drifted off to bed, Sam eagerly awaited to be praised by Laura. Yet as they moved around the apartment finished up the cleanup from the party, she remained silent.

"So how'd I do?" Sam finally asked when they were alone.

"How'd you do? I've never been so embarrassed in my life."

"Embarrassed? I do everything I can to keep from embarrassing you and you're still embarrassed? I didn't get into a single shouting match. No one stomped out of the place. Everyone had a good time. I don't get it."

"You deceived my friends. You lied to them. You said things I know you don't believe."

"I wanted to see what it was like to be a dead fish."

"What?"

"A dead fish. It's a paraphrase of Malcolm Muggeridge that I learned from my sister: 'Only a dead fish swims with the tide.' I never get to swim with the tide. I'm always the contrarian. Suppose I had been myself? Suppose, just for the sake of argument, I had also kept my cool. How am I going to defend capitalism when the businessman in the show endangers consumers with his product, buys off government officials and will do anything to make money? How am I going to argue against government regulation when the government official in this show is a saint in high heels, a gorgeous redhead who jogs to the Indigo Girls and who sacrifices a high salary in the private sector in order to pursue economic justice?" Sam stopped, his brow wrinkling in thought. "Was that Demi Moore?"

"No. It was Nicole Kidman." Laura's voice was quiet. She had been angry, but now she was calm. Why was Sam so worked up?

"Aren't you overreacting a little bit here, Sam? It's only a television show."

"I don't know what that means."

"Don't be silly, Sam. You know what I mean. It's not real. It's for—what's the phrase—entertainment purposes only."

"Really? Just a show? All right. Well then let's imagine a different kind of show. Suppose there were a television show called, oh, let's say, 'Class Dismissed.' It stars Jack Nicholson as a creepy English teacher in a rich suburban public school. He's rarely prepared for class, hates literature, and speaks ungrammatically. His notes are twenty years out of date. He often comes in with alcohol on his breath. He fondles his students and sleeps with the troubled ones who seek status or the reward of the higher grades he confers on them. If you don't sleep with him, he might lower your grade out of spite, but then again he's always willing to sell you a grade for money if the price is right. He's the union representative so no one fools with him. He makes sure that school reforms that might make him work harder get bogged down and never come to pass. He also coaches the football team. As a former Marine, he gets his kicks by verbally and physically abusing the poor performers. When students apply to college—" Sam stopped. "Why are you laughing?"

"The whole thing sounds more like a comedy. Maybe with, I don't know, Jim Carrey, not a sinister Jack Nicholson."

"Oh no. It's a gritty drama about a depraved man who wrecks young lives. It's gripping. People love it. They center their activities around it and tape it if they have to miss it for some reason. In the season finale, there's a student who threatens to go to the local paper with the teacher's shenanigans unless he helps him get into Harvard. So our friend has him murdered. Imagine watching that show, surrounded by a bunch of parents. At first, you laugh it off as absurd, just as you are doing now, but someone asks whether you have ever known a teacher who comes in with alcohol on his breath. Yes, you confess, there is Mr. Larkin, your colleague in English who sometimes stays out too late or starts too early. It's a departmental secret you try not to notice, but there it is. Then someone wants to know if you have ever known a teacher dismissed for sexual impropriety. You're in your first year of teaching so you don't know of anything personally, but of course you've heard of Mr. Mansfield, before your time, but this kind of gossip dies hard. He was forced out of the Edwards School four years ago and there was a 'settlement' with the girl's parents. And so it goes, down the line. Every depravity has a counterpart in your experience."

"But—"

"But to wrap all of this loathsomeness into one character is unfair, you explain."

"Well, yes," Laura said, "that's exactly what I was going to say."

"But it's just a show, your fellow viewers explain. In fact, the other viewers find it peculiar that you are so sensitive to this— what's the word?—*exaggerated* picture of the teaching profession. Don't take it so seriously, they say. But you do. It's hard not to when you realize that shows like this—and its imitators, which spring up in search of such high ratings—shows like this erode the respect people have for schools and teachers. You start to hear jokes at parties about your profession that are less than flattering. When you show annoyance and frustration, your friends look puzzled and explain it's just a joke."

"I'm sorry, Sam, but I still think it's harmless. It's just a way to pass the time."

"Maybe. Let's look at tonight's show, what was it called again?"

"Beauty and the Beast."

"Subtle. So did any of the earlier episodes show how the Beast treats his workers? A saint no doubt."

"Not exactly," Laura confessed. "Earlier in the season, there was a show about his decision to close down a factory in Ohio and open one in Mexico with lousy pay and dangerous conditions. The Mexican workers make about a dollar an hour while Krauss makes millions. Then later we found out that one of his company's pharmaceutical products doesn't work but he plans to market it anyway, endangering people's lives."

"Didn't this Grouse guy also murder his former secretary?"

"Well it looks that way. Heather Hathaway is in a coma. She might make it. She might not. And we don't know if Krauss is behind it yet. This was the season finale, so we'll have to wait until next season. It's Krauss, not Grouse, by the way. And I admit the murder thing *is* a little exaggerated."

"And the rest of it? The consumer deception, the abuse of workers, the generally obnoxious and repugnant personality of Mr. Krauss that I saw tonight? The rest of it you swallowed hook, line, and sinker as broadly representative of corporate America. You loved it. It confirmed your view of business and the essential goodness of government oversight. It let you revel in the consumer as victim and employee as victim."

Sam was right about one thing anyway, Laura admitted to herself. She loved the show. She loved Erica Baldwin.

"I recognize that some CEOs are less compassionate than Mother Teresa," Sam continued. "I understand that unbridled capitalism does not result in a life of delight for every citizen. I understand that there are people in the world like Charles Krauss. I recognize that some marketing schemes are dishonest. I recognize that some workers have a tough time. I recognize that the marketplace leads to imperfect outcomes. But the people on the other side of the issue, the people who sat here tonight who distrust and despise the marketplace, do they ever consider the costs of strangling competition via regulation? Do they ever notice the activities that never occur, the activities that go unseen because of regulation? Do they ever worry about the life-saving medical devices that don't get produced or discovered because of the cost of complying with the FDA? Do they ever miss the playgrounds and ice-skating rinks that don't get built because of the costs of liability insurance? Do they ever consider the possibility that the Erica Baldwins of the world are often less than saintly and care more about their own power than making the world a better place? So how do you think I feel sitting here watching a one-sided television show with people who not only disagree with my point of view but fail to even acknowledge that my point of view exists? Your friends here tonight can't imagine that a decent human being would favor a system that might allow a single Krauss to flourish. Because in their mind, all the CEOs are Krausses and the price of economic justice is eternal vigilance. Someone like myself, someone who believes that competition constrains the forces of greed, I'm—what's the word you used the other day?—I'm just a shill for Krauss. After all, we hold the same views, don't we? Obviously I like seeing children starve and workers oppressed."

"OK, Sam. Point taken. But what about George Sutherland?"

"You mean the guy from the small town in Ohio who works at the 7-11?"

"That's him. It may be a TV show, but there are still people like George Sutherland out there in the real world. People who lose their jobs. People with families."

"I feel sorry for the George Sutherlands of the world. I really do." Sam's voice was quiet now. The sarcasm and the outrage were gone.

"So how can you give the Krausses of the world free rein to ruin his life and so many like him?"

"Your premise is all wrong," Sam said calmly. "You make it sound like CEOs who close factories do it joyfully. When the CEO of AT&T fired 40,000 people, everybody blamed the greedy CEO. The real cause was the innovation of MCI and Sprint. It was their success that forced AT&T to become more efficient. It would be easy to keep jobs at AT&T. Outlaw competition from new rivals. But rivals force AT&T to improve service and lower their prices."

"The customer gets a good deal if he or she has a job. Workers end up on the short end of the deal."

"Sometimes workers lose their jobs and the result is hardship and suffering. But don't forget the 250,000 people at AT&T who kept their jobs. Without the changes, AT&T might not have been able to survive. Then there are the 100,000 workers at MCI and Sprint. They count too. If you want people to be motivated to change the world, you have to let the market reward their efforts.

Unfortunately, that means tolerating the negative side of competition as well."

"You call it 'the negative side' but thousands of people's lives are turned upside down by so-called downsizing. You make it sound like the CEO is the noble captain of the ship, valiantly fighting the storms of commerce. He tearfully sacrifices some of the sailors in order to save those that remain. But some captains are merely incompetent. And some are despots who cut people loose for the thrill or the extra profits."

"I know. I don't deny it. I think most do it mournfully, but never mind. I'll even defend those real-life CEOs, if there are any, who, like their television counterparts, coldly pull the plug on an American factory in order to improve the bottom line."

"Sam!"

"I'm serious. Krauss realized he could save money by shutting down the plant in Ohio and shifting the work to Mexico. That doesn't only happen on television. It happens in real life, too. Put yourself in Krauss's shoes. You are the CEO of a major multinational corporation. You have, let's say, 150,000 workers spread out over America and the world. You have thousands of stockholders. Many of them are retired or plan to retire using your company's profits as the wellspring for their retirement income. You are being told that you can save your company money by moving the plant to Mexico. You know it will hurt your workers in Ohio. Choose. Do you move the plant or keep it in Ohio?"

"Keep it in Ohio. A few extra dollars of profit aren't worth destroying the town of Matalon."

"Are you sure?"

"I'm sure. Especially if along with destroying the town in Ohio, I also exploit the Mexicans."

"So it would be better not to put any factories in Mexico?"

"No, I see that would hurt the Mexicans too. If there's going to be a plant in Mexico, I would at least make sure they make decent wages."

"I can imagine. So how much would decent wages be?" Sam asks.

"I don't know, maybe $5 an hour. And I'd make sure they had the same safety standards as the factory in America."

"And suppose at $5 an hour, and with all those safety costs, the workers there aren't productive enough to make the factory profitable? Would you be willing to drain profits from elsewhere in the company to subsidize the Mexicans?"

"Probably not. But anyway, it doesn't matter, I'd keep the plant in Ohio in the first place."

"I think it would matter to those Mexicans. Because of 'exploiters' like American multinationals, the wages there have risen steadily. Sure, they're poor by American standards, but they are on the right path. But you care more about people in Ohio than you do about Mexi—"

"Sam, you're twisting my argument."

"A little. Sorry. But let's focus on those Americans anyway. I think you said a few extra dollars of profit aren't worth destroying a town over."

"Something like that."

"How about a lot more profit? Does that make it easier or harder? Is there some point where you would destroy the town or should the factory stay there forever? The Soviets never closed factories, you know. Think what that does to the motivation of management and the workers. You know the favorite expression of the Soviet worker in the worker's paradise? 'We pretend to work and they pretend to pay us.' A lot of those factories are still open and still draining the Russian treasury because they can't cover their costs. So should the factory in Ohio just stay open forever?"

"That's an impossible question to answer, Sam. You're just—"

"An impossible question?" Sam interrupts. "You're the CEO. You have to answer questions like that every day. How do you decide?"

"I don't know. I just know that sometimes it's better to sacrifice profits for people."

"Sounds good. Unfortunately, your competitors don't have your, let us say, balanced view of life. They move their plants to cheaper, more efficient locations. They adopt new technology, even though it puts some workers out of work. They downsize when some divisions get fat. They become better than you at manufacturing and marketing. It sounds cutthroat, but your competitors are full of creative, innovative people who are using their skills to the utmost. And they are doing better than you. Because of their efforts, their prices are falling, benefiting consumers. They are hiring more workers at higher wages, bringing in new talent and luring away your best people. And your company, Compassion, Inc.? Your company has passed up opportunity after opportunity because, after all, your profits are big enough. You don't have to be greedy. But now your competition is charging lower prices than you and stealing your customers. You have to match those prices. You have no choice. At first, it just means lower profits. But eventually profits become negative. And stay negative. You go out of business. Your employees are looking for work. Those stockholders who were counting on you for their retirement, their nest egg is suddenly wiped out. What do you tell those employees and those stockholders? Who cares about people, now? You or your competitors?"

"You're cheating, Sam. You've just picked the worst case scenario to make my philosophy look rotten. You've—"

"I would say the writers for that television show have done the same thing with my philosophy. Plenty of successful capitalists don't have to downsize, don't have to shut down factories here in order to expand outside of America, but never mind. Give me your best case."

"Why can't I simply accept a slightly lower rate of profit? I don't want to run my factories like welfare programs. I just won't try to save every penny on every transaction."

"That's an interesting idea. If you're the owner of the business, then it's fine. The profits are yours. You're free to put them back in the business. You're free to hire a neighbor who is down on her luck and needs a job desperately even though you don't really need an extra worker. Remember what Aaron Feuerstein did?"

"No. Who's he?"

"He owns and runs Malden Mills. They invented and make Polartec, the stuff most fleece jackets are made of. When one of their plants in Massachusetts burned to the ground, Feuerstein paid for three months wages and four months of health benefits for the 1200 idled workers. It cost him over $10 million. Then he found work for most of them until he could build a new state-of-the-art mill. I love that story. What Feuerstein did was noble and generous. It was also good business, up to a point—he earned a lot of loyalty with his generosity. But I doubt he did it for the return and I doubt the return covered the $10 million. He did it because he's a religious man and he thought it was the right thing to do."

"That's a great story. That's true corporate responsibility."

"But he was spending his own money. When it's your business, you're free to give away your profits to charity. When it's your business, you're free to pay your workers more than the market will bear, not because it makes them better workers, but simply because you enjoy seeing them happy. It's your money. But ultimately, I think you would be hard-pressed to run a company that way. The world is uncertain. Unpredictable. Even ruthless CEOs find their profits suddenly going negative because something in the competitive landscape has shifted. Then you go broke. Out-of-business. Think of profits as the fuel that drives the entire enterprise. Without them, everything falls apart. The jobs, the wages, the pensions, the donations to community projects. Profits make everything possible. Without them, nothing is possible. Think of living in Siberia where your survival depends on finding enough wood to fuel the wood stove. Do you think you would ever feel like you had enough wood? Would you ever take chances with the wood you had and devote it to artwork?"

"But Sam, if another family came along without wood, wouldn't you share with them? Or would you keep it all for yourself? Why is selfishness the only path?"

"Selfishness has nothing to do with it. If a thousand people hired me to find their wood, if they trusted me to be the person who made sure that everyone in the group survives the winter, would it be right for me to give away the group's wood? That would be wrong. Immoral even. I hope I would give away some of my own wood that I receive in pay. After I'd distributed the wood to the families who depend on me, I hope I would encourage them to share some of their wood with others who are cold. But for me to give away the *group's* wood, or to be less than diligent in searching for wood? That would be irresponsible. That would jeopardize the entire enterprise."

"I don't know. It doesn't seem immoral to help someone else survive the winter."

"Then give away your own wood. Exhort your neighbors to be generous. But when we talk about a CEO of a corporation, the CEO is the steward, not the owner. The profits don't belong to the steward. It's the steward's job to dispense the profits wisely for the health of the entire enterprise. When a corporation excels and makes big profits, there are cries of outrage. The attackers always assume that profits are a sign of exploitation rather than excellence. Competitors whine to the Justice Department and demand antitrust action. Customers ask for lower prices. Workers ask for higher wages. After all, they complain, the company can 'afford it.' It's really just a rationale for begging. 'You have a lot of money. I'd like some, please.' Just once, I'd like to hear a corporate spokesperson when asked to defend the company's profits respond like this: 'We make high profits because consumers are wildly enthusiastic about our superior product at a price that provides value. We encourage all our competitors to try and match our performance. We encourage our customers to stay with us only as long as they are satisfied. If you are dissatisfied with some area of our performance, be it where we put our factories or how much we pay our workers or the prices we charge, we encourage you to start a rival enterprise and outperform us. We thank our customers for enjoying our products and allowing the current level of profit. We intend to use those profits to further improve our fine products and to reward our investors who took a chance on our risky venture. Thank you very much.'"

"So the bottom line is all that counts?"

"Yes. But if you think that means cruelty and ruthlessness, then I have wasted my time trying to show you how I feel. Ruthlessness is bad business. Look at your friend Charles Krauss. Does ruthlessness help HealthNet's bottom line? Krauss is probably going to jail for murder or attempted murder. That will be great for his company's stock. Funny how CEOs on television are always killing somebody. But I've never known a CEO to do it in real life. I guess they all get away with it."

"Come on, Sam."

"Then there's Krauss's criminal deceit of the FDA. Your friends told me that in an earlier episode, he shredded results from clinical trials that could have hampered his company. Do you think it will help profits to sell a drug that doesn't work or that's harmful?"

"Won't it boost profits in the short run?"

"The very short run. If HealthNet were a real company, it could be totally destroyed by faking drug results or selling a product that didn't work or was harmful. As soon as people found out that the company wasn't trustworthy, the profitability of all their other products would be jeopardized. The price of their stock would plummet."

"OK, so ruthlessness isn't necessarily compatible with profitability."

"But it's more than that. Good customer service is the road to profitability. Low prices are the road to profitability. Treating your workers well is the road to profitability."

"I doubt that's any consolation to George Sutherland. Whether he is fired because of ruthlessness or a compassionate steward trying to save the organization, he's still out of work. What would you say to him?"

"I wouldn't like to face George. And while I think the portrayal of Krauss was over the top, there are plenty of George Sutherlands out there in the real world, people who have to deal with adversity and pain. Remember, I admitted to you a long time ago that even a perfect system will have imperfect outcomes. If George confronted me, I wouldn't give him a lecture on the beauty of the profit motive. And I wouldn't tell him his job had to go to preserve the other 100,000 workers in the company. I'm not that cruel or foolish. If I had to talk to him, I would try to get him to see that he wouldn't like living in a world where the factory in Matalon stays there forever, along with every other factory in every other town."

"How long do you think that conversation would take, Sam?"

"Not very long. I've met a few George Sutherlands in my life. Most of them are angry and not real interested in economics. I don't blame them. They just want their jobs back. I understand that, too. But if he wanted to hear me out, I'd talk to him about his children. Does he have any on the show?"

"Yes. We saw his wife with them while she was interviewed on television."

"I'm sure it was a poignant scene. But let's see what's going to happen to those kids. I'm sure George is concerned about them. If the factory were still there, they'd probably go straight into the factory out of high school, like their Dad probably did."

"Is there something wrong with that?"

"No, but I always ask my students if they want to be in the same occupation as their parents. Most of them say no. I doubt the Sutherland kids would be any different. Anyway, with the factory gone, they'll probably go to college—"

"How are they going to afford college? Their dad works at a 7-11."

"Well, they probably won't be going to Stanford unless they get a scholarship or a lot of loans. They'll end up at Ohio State or a community college. With the factory gone, the kids will have to invest in a different set of skills. But that is only half the story. Even with the factory protected by some government regulation, the Sutherland children could always choose an alternative career. The real key is that the alternatives available to those kids will be better because the factory has closed. Because factories get moved to Mexico and others are shut down, capital and creativity are unleashed to open up new fields, new jobs and new opportunities. We see the hardship caused by the factories that close. We don't see the connection between that hardship and new opportunity."

Laura sat quietly, listening to Sam. He was pacing now, his arms waving with excitement as he tried to get her to see his point.

"One hundred years ago," he continued, "over forty percent of the American labor force was in farming. Now it's less than three percent. Imagine a heart-rending television show about the kids at the turn of the century being driven off the farm by technology that improved farm productivity. Do you think those kids and their children today are glad that we let that happen? Imagine how impoverished our lives would be today if we had decided to stop changes in farming out of 'compassion.' The same thing has happened over the last fifty years with manufacturing jobs. We have replaced those jobs with opportunities in computers, information technology, telecommunications, and the myriad of new industries of American excellence. Imagine how much poorer we would be if we insisted on keeping all the jobs in manufacturing from 1950 and not letting those factories close. Imagine how the kids of today would feel if we told them that most of the job opportunities for them were in a factory. The jobs and opportunities that have arisen outside of manufacturing would never have occurred if we had created laws to maintain the status quo."

"But is it worth destroying the Matalons of America in the name of progress?"

"It's not in the name of progress. It's in the name of giving the children of the next generation the chance to use their skills to the utmost. Not in order to make them richer, though they will be, but in order to give them a chance to forge whatever kind of lives for themselves that they choose. The destruction of Matalon and other small towns only tells the ugly part of the story. One reason they are poorer is that the children of those displaced workers have left town in search of other, better opportunities. If you want to measure the full impact of change on those towns, you would have to gather in those children and measure their well-being in the world of new opportunity they have chosen to explore. Think about 'It's a Wonderful Life.' Do you remember what happens to Bedford Falls when George Bailey was never born?"

"Sure. It becomes this garish creepy place, real sleezy, lots of neon signs."

"That's right—it's called Potterville. That was Capra's vision of the worst thing that could happen to idyllic Bedford Falls. Well there aren't many Bedford Falls left in America, but they weren't destroyed by greedy bankers like Potter. They were destroyed by the George Baileys who escaped and found their dreams in the bigger cities."

"You know what the difference is between us, Sam?"

"Where shall I start?"

"Sorry. It was a rhetorical question. The difference between the two of us is that you care about the winners and I care about the losers. You want to make sure that the gifted have a chance to use their gifts. But not everyone is gifted. I want a world where there is a place for the losers as well."

"So do I, Laura. So do I." Sam was almost pleading. "But I don't accept the dichotomy between winners and losers. The world is not an egalitarian place. Some people are more gifted than others. Maybe I over-romanticize the way that capitalism gives talented people a chance to thrive. But the gifted folk don't thrive at the expense of those who are less gifted. Capitalism forces the gifted to share their gifts with others. Look at Sam Walton who started Wal-Mart. He had a lot of gifts—a passion to transform the world, an attention to detail, the ability to create a unique informal corporate culture, a realization that small towns and rural areas had room for another retailer, and what is often forgotten, an understanding of the power of technology to keep costs low and continually push them lower. Using those gifts made him a billionaire. But where did those billions come from?"

"From his customers."

"That's right. But his profit wasn't their loss. Paradoxically, his profit was their gain also. To get them into his store and to keep them as customers, he had to give them a better deal than they could get elsewhere. He gave them low prices. That freed up the money they once spent on clothes and sheets and toothpaste to spend instead on their kids or on vacations or health care or on savings for their retirement. And Wal-Mart's competitors learned how to achieve the same low prices for their customers if they wanted to stay in business. So the benefits that flowed from Walton's gifts extended even beyond his own customers."

"But not all his competitors stayed in business." Laura countered. "Wal-Mart destroyed a lot of small merchants on Main Street. Wal-Mart is another reason there are fewer Bedford Falls than there used to be."

"That's true. But I care more about the people than the towns. Who put those merchants out of business? It's easy to blame Wal-Mart. But Wal-Mart couldn't and didn't force people to become their customers. Wal-Mart had to earn their business. Evidently the people who lived in those small towns preferred to shop at those big ugly boxy Wal-Marts on the edge of town rather than those quaint little stores on the town square. Their preference made Sam Walton rich. And at the same time, he made his customers wealthier by giving them a better deal than they had before. His riches weren't taken from anybody. That's why I hate it when people say that successful capitalists or corporations should give something back."

"I thought you liked private charity, Sam."

"I do. And I think it's lovely when wealthy people give their wealth away. There's nothing wrong with the concept of 'giving something.' It's the extra word 'back' that drives me nuts. It implies that the wealth was stolen, that it once belonged to the community and should be returned. That's what got me even more upset when I was talking to your brother the other night. Sam Walton wasn't some kind of pirate or marauder. He added to the wealth of America. He didn't just shuffle it around. And the millions of customers who benefited along with him weren't on Fifth Avenue or Rodeo Drive. They were ordinary everyday people who flocked to his stores in search of low prices. That's why it's misleading to talk about winners and losers. The real choice isn't between winners and losers. It's not between compassion and heartlessness. The real choice is between a static and a dynamic world. A world where people are encouraged to be content with what they have, and a world where people are encouraged to dream of what might be. I know which world I want to live in."

Sam sat down. He was worn out. Laura was lost in thought.

"So why couldn't you say that to my friends?" she said finally. "You don't know how hard it was watching you pretend to be something you're not."

"Do you think it was easy for me? Look, Laura, we've known each other for maybe six months. I'm sorry I deceived your friends. But I did it to maintain our relationship, not to damage it. There's no way in thirty seconds or even in an hour of intense conversation I could convince them that I'm not cut from the same cloth as Charles Krauss. Let alone that my view of the world might lead to a world worth living in. What would I do? Tell them about the porch at my parent's house? Tell them about the fisherman in hell? Tell them about the power of competition? I need six months to be understood, not sixty minutes."

"I don't know, Sam. You really think six months is sufficient?"

Sam looked puzzled for a moment. Then he began to laugh. All of the tension wound up inside him uncoiled. He rolled off the couch and lay on the floor, spread-eagled.

"I give up," he said, still laughing. "You've slain me."

Laura poked Sam in the belly with a stockinged foot.

"Get up, lazybones."

Sam looked up at Laura. She was smiling at him, her toe still hovering over his midsection. A great joy ran through him. He was falling in love with this woman. But what was a man to do about it, under the circumstances? He didn't know, but he decided that a stockinged foot on your belly was some sort of invitation. He tugged on it. She protested, but she was giggling. Finally, she toppled to the floor and lay next to him. Raising himself up on an elbow, he leaned over and kissed her softly on the lips. And then he kissed her again, a little longer this time.

"Thank you," he said.

"For what?"

"For everything."

Laura smiled, then took a deep breath and stood up.

"Sorry, Sam, but I've got to throw you out. It's late and we working girls have to get our beauty sleep."

"OK, OK. I'm teaching tomorrow, too."

Sam headed out into the night. It had cooled off. He stopped at the bridge over Rock Creek Park and let the breeze play over his face. A pale yellow moon, nearly full, was rising above the trees. Emotion surged though him—a bittersweet cocktail of joy and sadness. He kept thinking of Laura, but he couldn't forget that tomorrow was his last class and his future, uncertain.

Laura lay in bed, struggling to fall asleep. It wasn't just the lateness of the hour that had made her push Sam out. She wasn't sure if she was eager for romance with Sam. They were so different. And maybe he was leaving the Edwards School. She wasn't sure how she felt. But she knew she didn't want him to leave. She had to find out what was going on with his appeal. Was he really going to be fired? Without a fight? From what she knew of Sam, she found it hard to believe he would go gently into that good night.

Eighteen LAST CLASS

The students in Sam Gordon's course, "The World of Economics," talked quietly among themselves waiting for Sam's appearance. The last class of a senior elective is usually boisterous. But the students were subdued as they waited. They all had heard rumors that Sam was leaving the Edwards School.

When Sam walked into his classroom for the last time, he looked uncharacteristically tired. His face showed a lack of sleep. His whole body seemed to be moving in slow motion compared to his usual pace. Taking a deep breath, he tried to stir up some energy within himself.

"Today we are going to look at one last area of government regulation, environmental regulation. Based on what you know about my views on public policy, do you think I am against environmental regulation or for it?"

"Against!" came the student chorus.

Sam had turned toward the blackboard. Now he wheeled around and faced the class.

"Gotcha!"

The joy of the surprise energized him.

"When people buy and sell from each other," he continued, "the transaction is voluntary. Both sides benefit or they take their business elsewhere. But when a polluter dumps toxic waste into a river or into the air, the people who want to drink the water or breathe the air receive the pollution against their will. It's a form of theft of the air and water. The key to good environmental regulation is giving people a way to deal with each other voluntarily. If you can do that, you have a chance to harness self-interest rather than work against it. Anyone know how Europeans came to Australia?"

"By boat," came a voice from the back.

"Ah, a comedian. Thank you, Jason. Yes, they came by boat. But the interesting point is that many came as prisoners. In the eighteenth and nineteenth centuries, the English exported boatloads of convicts to Australia. They were not resort cruises.

Sometimes as many as a third of the prisoners died on the way. This horrified a lot of law-abiding English citizens. Either out of guilt or love, they wanted to see lower mortality on those trips. So what would you recommend?"

Students raised their hands. One suggested better nutrition. Another, better medical care. Another suggested less crowded boats.

"Okay," Sam said, "But it's costly to feed the prisoners or give them better medical care or to carry fewer prisoners per trip. You can imagine that the milk of human kindness didn't flow plentifully through the veins of the average captain. In fact, some captains hoarded the food meant for the prisoners, let them die, and then sold the food when they got to Australia. Lovely fellows, weren't they? So I can't see them taking too eagerly to your suggestions for saving lives. Let's try an alternative. Let's force those captains to act more humanely. Let's pass legislation setting out minimum standards for food and medical care. Let's call that the Heavy Hand solution. Would that work? Britanny?"

"You'd probably have to put a government official on the boat to make sure that the captain kept the rules."

"And you'd have to make sure that the official didn't take bribes or get intimidated by tough captains," Sam added. "So the legislative solution might be fine in theory but it might not work so well in practice. What do you think an economist would recommend? OK, I've left out a key piece to the puzzle. In the early days of the prisoner transports, the government paid the private shippers on a per-prisoner basis. They paid them enough to cover the cost of food and medical care. Someone finally had the bright idea of paying them on the basis of how many prisoners got off the ship in Australia rather than how many got on in England."

Sam paused to let the students absorb the lesson.

"Isn't that a simple, brilliant, cost-effective way to bring about change? Call it the Light Touch solution. Harness the self-interest of the captains rather than legislate against it. It's about as close as you can come to a self-monitoring system. Rather than the government having to pay someone to keep an eye on the captain, give the captain the incentive to do the job himself. Rather than the government figuring out how much food and medical care it takes to keep a prisoner alive, let the captain, who is on the scene, figure it out. Sounds great, right? But it's even better. Under the Light Touch solution, the captains have an incentive to discover new, better and cheaper ways of keeping prisoners alive. Maybe give the prisoners more space. You take fewer prisoners but more of them survive. Maybe there are new medicines to try that discourage illness at sea. Maybe certain foods are better than others for keeping the prisoners healthy. If the captains reap the benefits, they have an incentive to constantly improve survival on the ships. And they have the information to keep that improvement going. No one else does."

"What's this have to do with the environment?" someone asked.

"A lot of environmental legislation is Heavy Hand. Here's an example—the government decides the best way to reduce air pollution rather than giving companies the incentive to discover it for themselves. And like the ship captains, the companies usually have a lot more information than the government. The government used to force power plants to install devices called scrubbers to clean up sulfur dioxide coming out of their smoke-stacks. Scrubbers were expensive—they could cost over $100 million. That was OK. Most or all of those costs got passed on to the users. That was good. It discouraged people from using power that dirtied the air. But are scrubbers the best way to get rid of the toxins coming out of smokestacks? They may have been at the time. But it's like telling captains the best way to keep prisoners alive—even if it's the wisest policy at the time, there's no incentive for improvement. Eventually, the government passed the ultimate Light Touch solution for controlling sulfur dioxide. The government decreed that if you wanted to emit sulfur dioxide you had to have a permit for each ton you emitted."

"How many permits were issued?"

"Good question. Each power plant got a fraction of what they had emitted before. So now they had to scramble. They had to figure out ways to emit less sulfur dioxide. The alternative was to buy permits from another power plant that had cut emissions enough to have permits left over. So the law implicitly imposed a fine on firms that didn't innovate and rewarded those who did. Not surprisingly, those incentives had a powerful impact on the amount of sulfur dioxide emitted. And power plants had an incentive to continue to look for cheaper ways to clean up the air. Not everyone was pleased with the result. Some environmentalists thought it was great, but others were morally opposed to the very idea of being able to buy the right to pollute. To some environmentalists, pollution is a sin rather than the inevitable cost of economic activity."

Sam stopped and looked out the window. His concentration seemed to fade for a moment. Then he snapped back into focus.

"Do you ever worry about chickens going extinct?" he asked the class.

The class laughed, wondering what he was talking about.

"Yes, Jason?"

"I'm going to guess that chickens are like pistachios. Just like we're never going to run out of oil, we're never going to run out of chickens."

"Nice try, Jason, but the economics isn't quite the same. But I'm always glad when someone remembers the Nut Room. Do you know how many chickens there are in America right now? OK, I don't either, but it's more than a billion. A billion. Jason had the right idea—chickens are not going extinct any time soon. But why? We're in danger of running out of peregrine falcons. So why are chickens numerous but peregrine falcons rare? Why are there plenty of cows but not enough whales? The simple answer is that unlike falcons and whales, you can own chickens and cows and keep them fenced in. Just as importantly, people have a reason to own them, raise them, and take care of them. Resources that are not owned by anyone get abused. The air. The oceans. The whales that swim there. You know I'm often skeptical of the benefits of government regulation. That's because the economy is self-regulating. But at the heart of that self-regulation is private property. You spend your own money very carefully. You spend a friend's money less carefully. You spend a stranger's money much less carefully. Why? Because of risk and reward. When you spend your own money, you bear the risk and you reap the reward. But when ownership is not clearly defined, the incentives of the marketplace disappear and the case for regulation becomes more compelling. So is there a way to treat whales like chickens?"

Sam stopped and looked up at the ceiling. The class took his question to be rhetorical and waited for his answer.

"Seems impossible," he continued, "but in Zimbabwe, they've found a way to let villages own elephants. Not the way you own a chicken. They give villagers the right to charge tourists for the right to look at the elephants in their region. They can also charge hunters for the right to kill an elephant. They—"

"That's disgusting," a student muttered.

"Which," asked Sam, "the shooting or encouraging people to shoot them?"

"Both. How could it help elephants to encourage people to kill them?"

"It's working for chickens. People like to eat chickens and that gives farmers the incentive to raise them and take care of them. It's a paradox—you'd think people eating chickens would reduce the chicken population. But I know what you mean. It does seem disgusting to let people kill an elephant. I love them. I think they're beautiful. Should someone be allowed to pay for the privilege of killing one? Seems horrible, doesn't it? But when villagers can benefit from living elephants instead of dead ones, their incentives change. They want elephants to become more numerous. That lets them charge more to tourists or hunters. So they set aside more land for habitat. They cooperate with the police to stop poaching."

"What's the difference between poaching and hunting?" the student asked. "In either case the elephant is dead."

"But the total number of elephants can be very different in the two situations. A poacher will try to kill every animal he comes across. But if a village has the rights to the elephants in a particular region, the villagers don't want every elephant hunted. That's the road to short-run profit and long-run ruin. In Zimbabwe, they started ownership programs in the mid-1970s. Even though hunting was allowed, Zimbabwe's elephant population rose at a time when the total in Africa as a whole was cut in half by poaching. And villages that were near starvation have been able to build schools and health clinics with the money they've earned. Not everybody is happy. Some environmentalists oppose the Zimbabwe program because they think hunting is immoral. It may be, but it depends what you care about. There are a lot more elephants in Zimbabwe as a result."

Sam stopped. He looked at his watch.

"We don't have much time left," he said. "I'm going to tell you a story and then I'll sum up the class. A few summers ago I was hiking with a couple of friends in Yellowstone Park, away from Old Faithful and the crowds, up by Montana. It was a perfect day—temperature in the low 60s, a few clouds in the sky, snow-capped peaks on the horizon. It was the kind of day when you remember to be glad you're alive. We were walking through a stand of young pine trees when we crested a ridge and the valley opened up below us. A river wandered through it and beyond the river were soft hills rising into sharper ridges and then those mountains on the horizon. It was magnificent."

Sam stopped to remember the glory of it.

"Then off to our right, we heard something move. A group of elk, maybe ten of them, were foraging among the pine trees. They looked as surprised to see us as we were to see them. They stared at us for a moment then trotted off. We watched those gorgeous animals until they disappeared among the trees. Seeing those elk gave the whole day a different flavor. They reminded us that we were walking in more than just a postcard panorama. We were in a wilderness. Or so we thought."

Sam was pacing now. The class wondered what he meant.

"When I got back from that trip, I did some reading on Yellowstone that put that day in perspective. Back around 1900, the federal government worked to eliminate wolves from Yellowstone. It made local ranchers happy because no wolves wandered out of the park to kill their livestock. And it calmed any fears that visitors to the park might have about vicious or rabid wolves attacking them or their kids. By the 1930s, the wolves were gone. In the meanwhile, with fewer wolves or none at all, the elk population grew. And grew. And grew. Park officials liked that. Visitors to the park would be more likely to see something wild and alive on their trips to the park. Just like I did."

Sam stopped and thought for a moment, searching for the right words. "When you tamper with a complex system," he said, "things happen you can't predict. One of the consequences was obvious—as the elk got more numerous, grazing by the elk got a lot more intense. The elk stripped the vegetation from the edges of the streams—bushes and shrubs and small trees, the willow and aspen that grow at the water's edge. Beavers need willow and aspen for food. So one of the unanticipated effects of getting rid of the wolves in Yellowstone was that the beaver population plummeted. Here's the irony. Wolves eat beavers. So you'd think that getting rid of wolves would be good for beaver. But the exact opposite turned out to be the case."

Sam shook his head.

"In 1995, the government finally reintroduced wolves into Yellowstone. I guess the American people have acquired a bigger taste for real wilderness. There are now about 120 wolves there. But even if the wolves reduce the size of the elk herd in the park, it's too late for the beaver. They'd have to be reintroduced artificially along with a massive reconstruction of habitat."

Sam stopped to let the lesson sink in.

"On the first day of class," he continued, "I told you to remember the pistachio nuts. I wanted you to remember the power of incentives to solve problems. On the last day of class, I want you to remember the elk. When you tamper with incentives, beware of the unforeseen. Our intentions may be good, but if we forget about the incentives that are woven through complex systems, we make terrible mistakes. It's bad enough to mess up the beavers in Yellowstone and turn a wild treasure into an oversized elk farm. But with economic policy, we play with people's lives. A lot of times, the consequences are not just unintended, but perverse. And the harmful consequences are often hard to see. Just like that day in the park when I enjoyed the elk. I didn't see the beaver that were missing. A lot of economic regulation works the same way. The unseen costs often fall on the very people it is trying to help. Look for policies that work, not policies that create the illusion you're making a difference. And if you want to be a good economist, always look for the unseen."

Sam stopped and looked at the clock. Only a few minutes left.

"That's a good place to stop and sum up the class. I know you'll forget a lot of what you've learned in here.

Some of the students laughed.

"I'm serious. It's the nature of the brain. But I hope there are a few things you'll remember down the road. We've talked a lot about the power of the marketplace—how competition channels self-interest to improve the world. Most people focus on the material side of the marketplace—capitalism makes us wealthy. But one thing I hope you'll remember—money isn't everything. I know that sounds funny coming from an economist. But economics isn't about money, it's about whatever gives you satisfaction and makes you content. At the individual level, that means that the salary is not always the best thing about a job. Everything else equal, higher pay is better, of course. But usually not everything else is the same about two jobs. What also matters is whether the job gives you the chance to learn and grow and what kinds of achievements the job allows and the satisfactions those achievements provide. The same is true for the marketplace as a whole."

Sam stopped pacing and sat on the desk, facing the students. He waited for a moment to make sure they realized the importance of what followed.

"Capitalism makes us rich," he said. "But that's not why I love it. The marketplace, unfettered by government regulation but fettered by competition, gives each of us a chance to transform the world in the way we wish. For some of us, that might mean simply making a living and providing for our families. For others, it means bringing new unimagined products to the world that transform people's lives. But whatever it is, the money side is almost secondary. It's the ability of the market to let us feel alive as a free people making our own choices as we go through life. Some people imagine that as a lonely life of struggle, of success and failure. But there's nothing about it that has to be lonely. Just because individuals make their own choices doesn't mean they're self-sufficient. It doesn't rule out love or charity or a sense of community. It's just that all those things are voluntarily created by the web of connections each of us weaves."

Sam stopped and paced for a moment.

"Finally," he said, "I hope you have learned the importance of respecting other people's choices. You know more about yourself than I can ever hope to know. I believe this gives you the right to live your life as you see fit, as long as your actions are peaceful. That means respecting my choices even when you think you may know better. I believe this is a fundamental principle of humanity, the right to be treated by others as an adult and not a child. As teenagers, you are in the last days of your apprenticeship before adulthood. Enjoy the freedom you will soon have. Use it wisely."

Sam stopped and walked over to the window. The window faced the courtyard where students would sit when the weather was nice. It was the same courtyard where Sam and Laura had talked about "Ulysses." Sam appeared to be looking at the very bench where the two of them had sat, but in fact his gaze went far beyond there.

"Economics is a way of looking at the world," Sam continued, turning back to the class. "It constantly reminds us that there is no free lunch. Every road taken means a road left unexplored. That can lead to regret. But choice is good. I am grateful to live in a world without free lunches. A world without consequences and costs is a world without meaningful choice. A life without responsibility is not the life of the adult—it's the life of the animal, the child, or the robot."

Sam stopped again and he sat down on the desk. He looked out at the class. They were good kids. He loved teaching them.

"I've recently made a number of choices about my own life and my career here at the Edwards School."

The bell rang, ending the period. No one moved.

"I want you to know what's going on," Sam continued. "I'm going to be leaving the Edwards School. I'm sure there's been speculation about why. It's over a disagreement about principle. I can't tell you any more than that. I *can* tell you I've loved teaching this class and the others here at the school."

Emotion finally got the better of him and he stopped to keep his voice from breaking. "I'll miss you," he said, looking out into their faces. Then he looked down and began to neaten up the papers on his desk.

The class sat in silence. They wanted to ask a thousand questions but it was clear from Sam's face that now was not the time. Sam looked up, as if surprised to see them still sitting there. "You can go," he said with a smile. They started to file out quietly.

"Amy," Sam said, "would you please stay after class for a moment?"

After everyone else had left, Amy sat down in the front row and Sam sat on the edge of his desk.

"A few months ago, someone left me a gift," Sam began. "I know the giver meant well. But it's a gift I can't accept. I'm sorry it has taken me so long to return it."

Sam held out an envelope.

"I didn't mean to put you in an awkward position," Amy said, taking the envelope. "I know my father has something to do with you leaving. I thought those receipts would embarrass him. I thought they would help you fight him." She was near tears.

"I think they would have helped. But those receipts don't belong to me. I'm sorry."

"But why won't you fight?" She was crying now.

"Because this is a fight I can't win. It's a fight I don't want to win. The real fight, the one over ideas, I'll fight that one forever. And as you grow older, and read some more and think some more, I hope you'll still be on my side. You are a very bright kid. I expect great things from you. Stay in touch, OK? I'll leave a forwarding address with the school once I know where I'm going."

Amy pulled herself together. "OK. Thanks for everything."

After she had gone, Sam lingered in his classroom. He sat down behind his desk, put his feet up, hands behind his head, and thought of all the good times. Then slowly he began to clean out his desk.

Nineteen REPAIRING THE WORLD

"'I have sworn upon the altar of God eternal hostility to any tyranny over the mind of man.' Another nice motto, don't you think?"

Sam and Laura sat on a bench at the Tidal Basin, a few hundred yards from the Jefferson Memorial, having a picnic lunch. The bench faced the Memorial. To the left was the towering obelisk of the Washington Monument. And further to the left, shrouded in the trees, the low profile of the White House. It was early June. Sam and Laura had submitted their grades that morning. Graduation was the coming Sunday.

"It's not a bad summary of Jefferson's worldview," Sam added.

"Where's it from?"

"I don't know. It's carved in stone, there," Sam said pointing at the Memorial. "You can miss it if you don't look carefully. It's inscribed on the inside edge of the dome, way up high. This is one of my favorite places," Sam said, leaning back against the bench and gazing across the water.

"That surprises me, Sam. Here we are in the heart of government power, looking at its religious monuments. I thought you were the great skeptic of government power."

"True. But I love America. It's still the place of possibility, the best place to dream of what might be. And that's because of a deeply held conviction many Americans have in the power of being left to one's own devices. The power of liberty to unleash the human spirit and let it soar. Besides, see the Capitol Building?" Sam pointed. "That's where most of the mischief gets started and finished. Look how the Jefferson Memorial looms over it because the Capitol is off in the distance. I like that." Sam stopped. "Let me show you something. You have to stand in the right place."

Sam and Laura walked maybe twenty paces along the Tidal Basin. "Look," Sam said, pointing toward the Jefferson Memorial. From where she stood, Laura could see clean through the columns of the Memorial at Jefferson's likeness in bronze, larger than life, outlined against the sky. "It's as if he's watching over the city," Sam said. "I like that too. Jefferson helped enshrine liberty in the American consciousness. It is what the American Dream is all about. Not the dream of riches, but the dream of the pursuit of happiness as the individual perceives it. I love sitting here and thinking about that."

"I've never been at this spot before. It's lovely." She looked around at the cherry trees leaning toward the water, the branches angling over their heads, almost protectively. "It must be amazing when the cherry trees blossom."

"It's exquisite, but I like it better now. It's quieter. Fewer tourists." They returned to the bench and ate, enjoying the view. Finally, Sam broke the silence.

"I'm going to tell you everything," he said, turning to face her. "About my leaving the Edwards School. I'm not supposed to tell anyone what is going on, but you don't count as 'anyone' so I'm going to tell you. I don't believe in gossiping so I hope you can keep it to yourself. It's a petty story. It still makes me angry, but I've made my peace with it."

"I'm listening. And I'll keep it to myself."

"Thanks. OK, here's what happened. You know Amy Hunt?"

"Sure, bright as a tack, volleyball star, Dad's a Senator, glorious blond—" Laura stopped.

Sam saw the look of concern on her face.

"Don't worry. Amy's not the problem. Not directly anyway. It's her father, Senator Hunt, long-time progressive in good standing. He's on the board of the school. He's a big-time donor and people pay attention to him. They should. He's a powerful man. Well, as far as I can tell, he put pressure on the administration to terminate my contract."

"Because?"

"I don't know why exactly, but I have a pretty good idea. I don't think he likes what I've been teaching his daughter. She's become a—I don't know exactly what to call it—"

"A free-market romantic?"

"Yep. What used to be called a classical liberal. A believer in the power of decentralized unplanned decision making by individuals. Unlike her Dad, who's an interventionist, a central planner, a paternalist. You know him."

"I like him. Or at least I did. Why do you think it's his doing?"

"The administration conducted an 'investigation,' based on complaints about my teaching. They interviewed a bunch of students in my classes and focused on questions of 'imbalance,' I think they called it. I'm sure the students mentioned my skepticism about government regulation. But you know that's not all I teach them. I try to teach them how to think. How to use economics to look at the world around them. But I do have a skeptical view of government, and the investigation seemed to have centered on that. The conclusion was that I was proselytizing for a particular ideology."

"That's ridiculous, Sam."

"My theory or their charge?"

"Their charge. Every teacher brings his or her philosophy to bear in the classroom. I do it with Wordsworth and with Dickens. Every political science and history teacher does it."

"I know. But I go against the grain. Most if not all of the board holds to a different philosophy. I'm an apostate. A heretic. And I made a couple of jokes I shouldn't have. I poked fun at some so-called caring legislation because I thought it would hurt the people it was designed to help. I should have kept my mouth shut. Those jokes got repeated to the powers that be."

"So you're going to fight it, right? Appeal the decision?"

"No, I'm leaving the school. I'll go to graduation, say goodbye to my students, and find another job."

"Sam!" she fairly screamed. "It's not fair. You've got to fight it."

"I've thought about it for months. I've had two opportunities to fight it and I finally decided to reject them both. The first is the funny one. Late one night, actually it was the night of the debacle at your parents' place, someone left an anonymous package on my doorstep. Well, sort of anonymous. It was obviously from Amy. It was an envelope with charge receipts from her Dad's charge card—meals, hotel charges. I assume he was either cheating on his wife or the ultimate sin, consorting with tobacco lobbyists."

"Juicy."

"Too juicy. And remember, you're sworn to silence on this."

"I'm sworn."

"Here's a daughter who's a sponge in my class either because she's never heard what I'm telling her or maybe she's rebelling against a father she never sees or who is cheating on her mother. Who knows? Either way, the whole thing's a mess. On top of it all, blackmail is not exactly my modus operandi. How could I justify using stolen property to avenge a personal slight?"

"I call it more than a personal slight. I call it injustice."

"I don't go that far. I gave the receipts back to Amy."

"OK. Good decision there. That's a can of worms. But why not appeal?"

"I was tempted. There was a hearing scheduled before the board. There were a lot of nights I lay in bed imagining my brilliant oration on the power of intellectual freedom. But finally, I decided to cancel it."

"Intellectual freedom is what a good school is all about. You could have made the case. You could have saved your job."

"Agreed, but the goal of a hearing isn't eloquence. It's winning. I knew I wouldn't win. That only happens in the movies. I couldn't see Senator Hunt standing up at the end, wiping away tears and saying, 'I've lived my whole life as a lie. Come back to the Edwards School, son.'"

"But you could have made a statement of what you believe in. How could you let that go by?"

"I wasn't sure I could keep my cool. It's one thing to yell at your brother. It's another to yell at Senator Hunt and the other board members. I was afraid of making a fool of myself to no purpose."

"There's still another option. You could sue."

"On what grounds?"

"The whole thing's discriminatory."

"I don't think economists are protected by antidiscrimination legislation."

"But Jews are. You're Jewish, right?"

"Yes."

"You could claim that your firing was due to anti-Semitism."

"But that's a lie."

"You don't know that. You don't know the real reason. Maybe it was anti-Semitism."

chapter nineteen

"I doubt it. And either way, I don't believe in the law."

"What law?"

"Antidiscrimination law. Life is about discrimination."

"Sam!"

"I don't mean the bad kind, though the bad kind comes along with the package. When we pick our friends we discriminate. When we choose where to live we discriminate. Discrimination is choice—choosing some things and rejecting others. The Edwards School has rejected me. I've got to deal with it."

"But they rejected you for an unfair reason!"

"Doesn't matter. I believe they have the right to do so."

"But why? Why?"

"Because they know more about how to run a school than the government or a jury or an administrative panel of judges."

"But in this case the school's wrong. You're a great teacher."

"I think so. They don't. I'm not thrilled about it. I said I got angry. One of the accusations was that my class was 'pro-business.' That drives me crazy. I—"

"But you are pro-business."

"I am not! I'm pro-capitalism."

"What's the difference?"

"There's a huge difference. I honor what business accomplishes for our lives. I honor the role that profits play in spurring innovation. But profits are restrained by the marketplace. There is nothing inherently good about profits."

"I don't understand. You've told me that the bottom line is all that counts."

"I believe that businesses should strive to be profitable, rather than trying to serve some social cause. That striving creates new and cheaper products that transform our lives for the better. That striving drives businesses to serve their consumers and to treat their employees well. But that doesn't imply that as GM goes, so goes the nation. Or that regulations are good or bad because of their impact on corporate profits. When the minimum wage is in the news, it's treated as if a higher minimum wage is good because it helps workers but bad because it hurts business. But economists who oppose the minimum wage do so because they believe that the minimum wage prices low-skilled workers out of job opportunities. Economists who oppose safety regulations in the workplace don't believe in the value of protecting corporate profits. They oppose safety regulations because they believe that imposing a uniform standard of safety on all workers is like making all drivers use airbags. For some workers, the benefits may not be worth the costs. I'm against the minimum wage. I'm against safety regulation in the workplace for those reasons. I'm against tariffs and quotas even though they can increase profits of some American companies. I'm against subsidies to business, I'm in favor of environmental regulation as long as it's structured properly. I'm—"

"OK. Calm down."

"Sorry. I'm a fan of capitalism. And because I am a fan, I realized that my anger—caused either by being smeared as a pawn of business or by the unpleasantness of losing my job—my anger isn't relevant to the justice of the decision. It took me a while to calm down and factor that out of the equation. Once I did, I realized they had the right to make the call. And I think that's fair."

Sam paused as a pair of mallard ducks cruised serenely across the shimmering reflection of the Washington Monument.

"I thought economists weren't very good at 'fair,'" Laura said.

"We're not, in the way that most people define it. Most people define it as 'equal.' If you have something I don't have, then it's not fair. If you have a job that I want and don't have, that's not fair. If you make more money than I do, that's not fair. I don't agree with any of those definitions, but my disagreement has nothing to do with economics. It's a philosophical view. My definition of fair is 'by the rules.' The Boston Celtics won the NBA championship for eight years in a row. Some would call that unfair because they won more than their 'fair share,' where fair share is defined to be no more often than anyone else. I'd say it was fair because they played by the rules."

"But that's sports. This is your life."

"I signed a contract with the Edwards School. It gave them a right to fire me. And by the way, they are giving me a little bit of money for the privilege, as specified in the contract. That same contract gave me the right to walk away had I wished. I call that fair. I reject the entire notion that once I'm hired by the Edwards school, I am entitled to this job. If they don't want me here, they're entitled to get rid of me."

"But who is 'they?' There are a lot of people, myself for example, and the students and surely some members of the board who want you to stay."

"Agreed, but you have to have someone take responsibility for the school. That's the board and the principal. Once the government interferes with that process by giving me the right to stop the school from making its own choices, a whole set of other incentives are put into motion."

"I'm more pragmatic than you are, Sam. I'm willing to inter-fere with the system if the result is less discrimination."

"Are you a racist?"

"I hope not."

"Are you prejudiced against women?"

"Of course not."

"So how would you like it if the government made you spend fifteen percent of your money at minority-owned businesses or fifty percent at businesses owned by women? Does that seem fair to you? And of course you would have to keep extensive records of all your receipts to prove that you aren't a racist or a sexist."

Laura thought for a moment. A plane thundered behind them, about to land. Laura waited for it to pass.

"That might bug me," she answered. "I wouldn't like keep-ing track of all the receipts. It would be a nuisance. I might resent it. And I suppose a store that is entitled to shoppers may not do the best job serving its customers. Point taken. But isn't there a difference between where you shop and someone having trouble finding work because of the color of her skin?"

"I think you should be entitled to shop wherever you want and I think an employer should have the right to hire whoever he wants. And that includes the right, if it's your business, to hire all women or all African-Americans either because you think they make the best employees or out of compassion for past injustice. But I don't believe the government has a right to tell you how to spend your money as a customer or as an employer."

"I understand that point. But it seems different with employment."

"But why would you want to work at a place that didn't want you and that only hired you because of your gender or the color of your skin? Why would I want to work at the Edwards School if I knew that they didn't want me? Forget what the reason is. Why would I want to use the power of the law to force them to keep me on?"

"Maybe you'll feel differently if you can't find another job. Or if you had kids to support."

"Fair enough. In that case it might be harder for me to be cavalier about walking away from the Edwards School. But I think I'll find a job. There are a lot of schools out there. Some of them may actually find my philosophical views a plus. They may not be my favorite schools to work at. And if the Edwards School really was anti-Semitic or racist, there are other places where Jews and blacks are welcome. I don't believe you have a right or entitlement to a particular job at a particular place. When you use the courts to enforce my desire to work where I want, you break the connection between choices and rewards that is the essence of responsibility."

"Maybe, but I don't see being Jewish or favoring capitalism as really big handicaps in the job market. Skin color or gender are different. I don't know if you can appreciate what it's like to face sexism or racism."

"Maybe not. I agree that it's harder in some cases to be a woman or an African-American in the working world. But remember that the Edwards School is in competition with a myriad of other private and public schools. If it consistently hires poor teachers because the administration is prejudiced, the school will become worse and have trouble attracting students. It will pay a price. That's the way I like the system to enforce excellence."

"But the Edwards School is the best private school in the city. Its reputation is superb. It will take years of bad decisions before they pay a price. How can you let them get away with injustice in the meanwhile?"

"Because I don't think it's injustice. And I think it has become the best school in the city because it has been free to pursue excellence as its leaders and board see it. I don't feel good about interfering with that process. And if it is an injustice, it's the kind that's so clouded by the complexity of the human heart that it's not the kind you want to fight using the courts and the legal system. Any of your parents' friends ever get divorced?"

"Sure," Laura answered, wondering how this could have anything to do with the conversation.

"My mom used to say, 'the human heart has its reasons that reason cannot know.' When a couple divorces, people always speculate on whose fault it is. It's a silly question really. Even the participants, the husband and wife, can't answer that question even when they can step outside of their emotions. A divorce is the product of a thousand misused moments. But didn't she cheat on him? Yes. But didn't he drive her to it? Yes. And didn't he drive her to it because she was curt and unfriendly? Yes. And wasn't she curt and unfriendly because he was rude and overbearing and obnoxious, selfish and abusive? Yes. But she *did* cheat on him, didn't she? Yes. So whose fault was it? You could spend a lifetime of investigation and still not know whose fault it really was. The legal system is smart enough not to try and determine that level of fault."

"What's that have to do with discrimination?"

"Because discrimination is only a word that cannot begin to capture the complexity of the human heart or human inter-action. We have a pretty good idea of what a murder is. We have a pretty firm idea of when someone is dead. So when you charge someone with murder, it may be pretty difficult to prove it, but at least we know what we're trying to prove. But discrimination?"

"Come on, Sam. You know it when you see it."

"In the extreme cases, yes. But you can't separate those out from the more ambiguous ones. Once there is legislation with economic consequences, racists are not the only ones at risk. Every employer is at risk because discrimination is not always observable or measurable. Except in extreme cases, discrimina-tion is always ambiguous. That means that we spend immense quantities of resources on both sides of a discrimination case trying to uncover the truth about the human heart. Once you put the human heart on trial in the courtroom, you no longer catch just the guilty. If you pass a law against what is essentially a sin, even the saint gets nervous. Even good-hearted administrators and employers want to avoid lawsuits; they become very cautious in hiring, especially someone from a protected group, such as women, minorities, or the disabled. The reason is that the costs of firing that person are now much higher."

"Saints don't have to worry about the law."

"Sure they do. There's no prejudice meter. There is no way to prove that a firing wasn't due to prejudice. How could an impartial outside observer know whether the true cause is merit or discrimination? There is always a chance the court will rule that there is discrimination. Look at my case. Five minutes ago you told me that *I* could claim anti-Semitism as the reason for my firing. I'm a perfect example of what's wrong with antidiscrimination law. Whose fault is it that I got fired? Couldn't I have done a better job? Didn't I sometimes make snide remarks? Unfairly represent views opposed to mine on a policy debate? On top of it all, I'm a lousy administrator. I missed meetings, deadlines for handing in grades. You name it. Or maybe it was the school's fault. Maybe the school doesn't like free-market economists. Maybe, just maybe, the administration *is* a little anti-Semitic. No swastikas in the hallway, but was that a look of displeasure I saw on the face of the principal when I had to cancel class for Yom Kippur? And how about the rarity of rye bread in the school cafeteria? Is that a subtle cultural statement or merely an innocent cost-saving measure?"

"You're being silly."

"Yes, I am. But the point is you could spend a lifetime trying to decide the true cause of my firing and whether it was just or not. Look, Laura. I'm an economist. You're a lawyer. I don't mean literally. I mean in the way you look at the world. You're the offspring of lawyers. We look at the world in different ways."

"Don't I know it."

"I look at injustice very differently from you. That's why I said to you long ago that I hoped you wouldn't go to law school. Forgive me if I'm being unfair to the lawyer viewpoint, but you're an activist. You see a wrong? Right it. And how do you right wrongs? There ought to be a law. Legislation! But legislation is a very blunt instrument. It never merely rights wrongs. It creates a whole new set of wrongs as well."

"I agree. But to fight injustice I'm willing to take a chance. I'd rather be an activist than a—I don't know—a 'passivist.'"

"But not everything unpleasant should be against the law. Rudeness is exceedingly unpleasant but it's not against the law. Yet. Making it illegal would reduce rudeness. But it would also reduce a thousand other beneficial forms of human interaction because people would be afraid of being sued. Making rudeness illegal puts the courts and the hand of the law into our private lives with no guarantee that the truth will out. Selling cocaine is against the law. And making it illegal has done nothing for drug use other than to glamorize it and make it more profitable. Why not let an activity be legal but reviled? Why not use other methods of discouraging and reducing the actions that we see as reprehensible? I'm not a 'passivist' or whatever you want to call it. I don't believe in standing idly by."

"So tell me what I should do. I want to make the world a better place. I want to *do* something. I want to fight for a cause. I want to help people. That's why I want to go to law school. I can't just stand back and let nature take its course. I want to help make things better."

"There are a lot of ways to make the world a better place without using the political process or the law. You can start a business and hire people you think are disadvantaged. You can read to old folks at a nursing home. You can volunteer at a shelter for abused women. You can tutor a kid who can't figure math out. You can come up with a product or service that makes people's lives better. You can help market that product so that people find out about it. All of these make the world a better place, one person at a time, through voluntary action. I don't believe you make the world a better place by legislation. You're just as likely to harm as you are to help. And when you use legislation, you discourage the private actions that might do the job in a more effective way. We can use social pressure. By using social pressure we've made people uncomfortable littering. We have made smoking socially unacceptable. We can raise children wisely. There is religious instruction. Rather than forcing people to love their neighbor, we can teach and inspire people to judge each other by the content of their character and not the color of their skin. And when we're done, the result will be a truly better world, not one that merely looks more just on paper."

"This comes back to our old argument. I don't want to wait for people to become better. I'm not as patient as you."

"And I'm not as comfortable with coercion as you are. You heard that class of mine. I think the world would be a better place if people watched less television. But I don't think you make the world a better place by banning television any more than you make the world a better place by banning discrimination. I'm not even sure if the world would be a better place if we could find a gene for prejudice and remove it. Any more than we would be better off removing the gene for hate. I think we're here to overcome our natures. Legislation doesn't change our natures. It only deceives us into thinking we've repaired the world. Forcing people to hire women doesn't make them less sexist."

"It might. It might get them to adjust their views. It might educate them. They might find out that women can do a job they thought couldn't be done by a woman. You might get rid of some prejudice."

"That's true. There can be good consequences of people being forced to go against their nature. And there can be some horrific ones. It can create resentment that intensifies prejudice. It can cause the favored group to see themselves as victims. It can reduce the incentive for people to improve on their own. It can raise the costs of hiring the group we're trying to help."

"I guess we're back where we started, Sam. We see the world in different ways."

"Yes and no. We see the world in different ways, but I hope we're not back to where we were when we argued on that subway trip last fall. True, I'm not going to law school. And I haven't made you into a free-market romantic. But you're not opposing counsel. I'm not trying to win a debate. I just want you to understand that there is more than one way to repair the world."

Laura took Sam's hand and smiled.

"Let's take a walk," she said.

They strolled around the Tidal Basin over to the Jefferson Memorial. They admired the colossal statue of Jefferson and read all the quotes carved into the walls. They gawked at the gawking tourists who came from all over the country and the world. Then they went outside and sat on the steps that face the water.

"This isn't a bad view either," Laura marveled. "You lose the Capitol Building but you gain the Lincoln Memorial."

They sat and enjoyed the vista in silence. They weren't holding hands any longer, but Sam felt a connection beyond the immediate touch of Laura's hand. Her presence next to him gladdened his heart. He let the silence grow. Finally, she spoke.

"Thanks for telling me what's going on," she said. "Here's my confession. I love that you're a fish that swims upstream. But this thing at the school is one time I was hoping you'd swim with the tide and act like anybody else would and fight for your job. And not just because I think you deserve to stay. I'll miss you terribly if you're not at the Edwards School next year. Tell me you're going to at least stay in town."

"I want to. Now that we've mastered the ability to talk about the most contentious topics in a calm voice, I'd like to move on to some new areas of conversation. We could talk about poetry or Chinese cooking techniques, or the hills outside of Rome. I think we're ready. When can I see you again?"

Laura smiled at him.

"Saturday night, I hope, the skit show at school. I'm the advisor so I have to go. Will you come? The students made me promise I'd bring you."

Twenty SHOW TIME

Every year, the seniors at the Edwards School wrote and performed a satirical review of their senior year. Held in the school's main auditorium, it was usually a series of skits with the occasional song, the melody taken from somewhere else, the lyrics altered for humor. The skits poked fun at their teachers and the school administration. Being in Washington, D.C., they often made light of the political events of the year. Videotapes were made so the students could have another set of memories to go with their yearbooks.

The show was always held on the Saturday night before Sunday's graduation. Each year, a member of the faculty was assigned to advise the students. The advisor's main job was to keep out any cruel or tasteless material. Any musical or dramatic ability on the advisor's part was gravy. The job often went to the youngest member of the English department. Laura was this year's advisor.

Laura was only a few years older than the performing seniors. She had developed a great rapport with them. While she had little musical ability, she had helped the students hone their material with her feedback and comments.

When Sam and Laura arrived, the auditorium was packed with students and family members, in town for the next day's graduation. It was traditional for faculty and administration to stand in the back and take the mild abuse sent their way standing up. Most faculty viewed it as a badge of honor to be mentioned in a skit and see one's classroom style or accent imitated. It was usually a delightful evening.

But both Sam and Laura were nervous awaiting the start of the show. Laura wanted to see the show come off hitch-free. Sam, despite assurances from Laura that they had steered clear of controversy this year, was anxious about any possible mention of his situation.

The opening song, a medley on the political scandals of the past year, was greeted with laughter and applause from the crowd. Much of the audience was involved in the Washington political culture in one form or another. Sam enjoyed it immensely and

Laura was thrilled to see it going well. Then there were a number of skits lampooning the teaching styles of various faculty members.

The performances were high caliber; there were some very talented kids at the Edwards School. The last skit finished with a song about the highlights of the school year. When it was over, the applause went on and on. Amy Hunt, who had acted as the emcee for the entire show, went to the microphone and jubilantly called out over the crowd for Laura Silver to come up on stage. As the applause continued, Amy presented Laura with a bouquet of roses. The cast, in the middle of its curtain call, stopped to applaud Laura. Sam, standing in the back of the room, was proud to see the affection the students had for her.

Then Amy raised her hand and quieted the crowd.

"We'd like to do one more number as an encore," Amy said. "As you may have noticed, most of our songs tonight have been parodies of current hit songs off the radio. But this one is an old song, taken from the *Wizard of Oz*, our version of the Scarecrow's song, 'If I Only Had a Brain.' We dedicate it to the teaching wizard who took a bunch of brainless seniors and taught them that just like the Scarecrow, they really could learn to think for themselves. He is leaving the Edwards School and this is our farewell to him."

The whole cast came to the front of the stage. Laura stood off to the side unsure of what to do. She wanted to grab and Amy ask her what was going on, but she couldn't see a way of doing it gracefully. A feeling of deep fear came over her. Sam, too, felt his stomach churn. The music began and the cast sang in unison to the magical melody:

Once there used to be a teacher
Part economist, part preacher.
His class was quite a strain
Still we're sorry that he's leaving
And we surely have been grieving
With both sides of our brain

Some compare him to Attila
But there isn't a scintilla
Of truth in what they claim
Even though he likes linguini
He's no teaching Mussolini
For his views are rather tame

The music changed over to the wistful bridge of the song:

For he loved to make us think
He understood what school was for
Now they've pushed him to the brink
And they've kicked him out the door.

Then the music changed back to the main melody:

So our hat's off to Sam Gordon
The economics Michael Jordan
The Board must be insane
If they knew how much we loved him
They never would have shoved him
If they only had a brain.

The students in the audience cheered wildly. The parents and guests looked puzzled and confused. A furious Principal Harkin was fighting his way to the front of the room. He was on his way to grab the tape from the student running the video camera for the school. Every eye scanned the back of the room in search of Sam and his reaction. But he had fled long before the song's conclusion. So he also missed Amy's final words at the microphone.

"Everyone should know that this encore was a surprise. Laura Silver knew nothing about it. It was all our fault. But we're off to college!"

The students stepped off the stage to more applause and cheering. Laura, in tears, exited stage left.

Twenty-One SPARE CHANGE

Months later, on a sunny day in September, a self-assured young woman left the Edwards School on her way to run some errands. She headed toward the Woodley Park station of the Metro. Sitting at the entrance was a man with matted hair. Even though the temperature was in the upper 50s, he was wearing a heavy overcoat.

"Spare change? Have a good day. Spare change? Have a good day," he called.

The young woman stopped and seemed to be lost in thought. An observer might have thought she was trying to decide whether it was a good idea or not to make a donation. In fact, she was merely lost for a moment in a flood of memories of a man she once knew and the handful of intense conversations they had shared. Finally, she reached into her purse, took out a dollar bill and softly laid it in the beggar's hand. As she was about to get on the escalator, she heard a voice.

"Aren't you afraid he's going to waste it on drugs and alcohol?"

The young woman, whose auburn curls caught the sunlight and gave it substance, stopped suddenly. That voice. One she hadn't heard for what seemed longer than three months. She came ever so close to losing her composure. But she held on and turned to the man, a tall, lanky fellow. "I don't know, " she said. "I kind of hope he does."

"Harrumph," the man snorted. He went over to the chanting man with uplifted hands and dropped a can of V-8 juice into the man's hat.

"Sam!" Laura cried out in a mixture of exasperation and delight. "Where have you been?"

"Where have I been?" Sam asked, following Laura as she stutter-stepped onto the escalator. "For the last couple of afternoons I've been hanging out here at the Metro Station, V-8 juice in hand, hoping to surprise you. If you hadn't shown up today I'd have followed the more mundane strategy of calling."

"And the last three months? I've been desperate to let you know what happened on that last night at school. That encore wasn't my fault. I had nothing to do with it. I called. No answer. I went by your apartment. Nothing. So I gave up and wrote you a letter. But I never heard from you. Did you get it?"

"I just got it last week. I also got a copy of the videotape from Amy."

Laura's face lit up.

"Where did she get a copy? I thought Harkin kept that videotape to himself."

"He did, evidently. But there are a number of underground copies circulating among the students that were made by parents that night. In fact, I'm the proud owner of a copy of the Annual Edwards School Skit show filmed by none other than one Senator Hunt. He must have an expensive camera. It's an excellent video."

"So you got to hear Amy's disclaimer at the end!"

"I did. But you know the complexity of the truth, don't you?"

"Meaning?"

"How would a man know whether that disclaimer was said to shield the true instigator from detection? Maybe you were behind the whole thing after all."

"Oh, Sam. I'd never lie to you like that. Bring you to the show under false pretenses? That would be horrible. I'd—"

Sam raised a hand.

"What?" Laura asked.

"One of the advantages of the hand-held camera is you get that gritty hand-held look to the video. But another benefit is that you sometimes get a different camera angle from the official version. Because of where Senator Hunt was sitting in the auditorium, his video camera was able to capture, in addition to his daughter at center stage leading the students in that ghastly song, a young woman, really a rather beautiful young woman, offstage, in the wings, stage left. As I said, it was a very high quality image. She appeared to be crying—"

"Sam!"

"After repeated viewings, I concluded she actually *was* crying. Of course she could have been merely pretending to cry. But that's far-fetched, don't you think? Even for a conspiracy theorist."

The subway train arrived. Once again, as they had done a year before, Sam and Laura found themselves on a crowded Metro car, oblivious to the mass of travelers around them.

"I felt terrible, Sam. I'd promised you that you were going to be left out of the evening's festivities and you turn out to be the centerpiece. That song was as big a surprise to me as it was to you—though I thought it rather nice, actually. But when I saw you were gone, I felt miserable."

"I'm sorry I ran out on you. It was quite a run. I left town the next morning. I couldn't face graduation. I wasn't comfortable being a cause célèbre. It's just not my style. But I ran to Houston to hang out with my sister, not St. Louis where I had left my parents' address for forwarding. They were on vacation so the mail sat there for a while. That's why it took so long for Amy's tape and your letter to find me. It was a sweet letter. Given how long it took to get to me, I thought I'd answer it in person."

"I'm glad you did. It's great to see you. Are you sticking around?"

"I'm looking for work. I've got some substitute teaching jobs lined up for now. I'll be OK. I'm also hoping to woo this woman I used to know here. Auburn hair, delightful company, good-hearted but misguided."

"Give it up. Do you really think you have a chance with her? The two of you are like oil and water."

Sam saw the smile hovering at the corners of Laura's mouth. The subway doors opened and they stepped out into the station.

"I'm thinking maybe oil and vinegar," Sam said. "You have to work at keeping them together. I'm cautiously hopeful. It may take a while. But I'll keep at it 'till a' the seas gang dry, my dear, and the rocks melt wi' the sun.'"

"Robert Burns, isn't it?"

Sam nodded as they headed toward the exit.

"Have you been spending time with those poetry books again?" Laura asked.

"Naw. Just all summer. It does a man good to branch out, don't you think?"

And chatting about poetry and this and that, they emerged out of the long, dark shadows of the escalator tunnel and into the bright sunlight.

The interested reader may want to look further into the topics that Sam and Laura discuss. What follows are some classic works dealing with Sam's views on economics, politics, and political economy. This is followed by sources and references for specific topics in the book organized by chapter.

The Classics

The work of Milton and Rose Friedman is a good place to start for the reader interested in delving more deeply into the issues of fettered versus unfettered capitalism. *Free to Choose: A Personal Statement* (Harcourt Brace, reprint edition, 1990) is a good first choice. *Capitalism and Freedom* (University of Chicago Press, 1962), though a little more formal, is worth reading just for the fact that many of its suggested policies (which were thought by many to be crazy when the book was first published) have become well accepted by a wide range of policy makers.

After the Friedmans' work, I would recommend the work of Frederic Bastiat. Bastiat wrote 150 years ago, yet you can pick up almost anything he wrote and it seems like it was written for a policy debate in our times. A good place to start is "What Is Seen and What Is Not Seen" and "The Law" from *Selected Essays on Political Economy*. Then read *Economic Sophisms*. All are published by the Foundation for Economic Education (800-452-3518 or at www.fee.org, they can also be found on-line in their entirety at www.econlib.org).

Friederich Von Hayek, along with Milton Friedman, deserves much of the credit for sustaining the argument for liberty through the middle part of the twentieth century when authoritarianism was on the rise and the defenders of liberty were rare. While Hayek's style is not as lively as Friedman's or Bastiat's, I recommend *The Road to Serfdom* (University of Chicago Press, 50th anniversary edition, 1994) or *Individualism and Economic Order* (University of Chicago Press, reissue edition, 1996). In the latter, you will find the superb "The Use of Knowledge in Society," which explores the remarkable ability of markets to synthesize knowledge without central direction. A related theme is found in Leonard Read's delightful "I, Pencil," a brief fable on how economic activity gets coordinated without a coordinator. It is available from the Foundation for Economic Education along with Read's *Anything That's Peaceful*.

Adam Smith's discussion of the invisible hand and his insights into human nature and economics can be found in *An Inquiry into the Nature and Causes of The Wealth of Nations*. I also encourage the reader to look at Smith's *The Theory of Moral Sentiments* as an antidote to those who think Smith was a fan of greed or ruthlessness. You can find both on-line at www.econlib.org.

Running Out of Oil (Chapter One)

The numbers from Sam's quiz and his discussion of oil are taken from the *Oil and Gas Journal*, reprinted in *International Energy Statistics Sourcebook* (Pennwell, 1995) and the *BP Amoco Statistical Review of World Energy* (June 1999). The world consumption number in 1970 is actually production, which is usually a good approximation of consumption. Some analysts believe that the current reserves estimate of one trillion barrels may not be comparable to methods used in the past. I want to thank Mike Lynch of the Center for International Study at MIT for these numbers and helpful background. The interested reader may want to read *The Ultimate Resource 2* (Princeton University Press, revised edition, 1998) by Julian Simon for a look at how human creativity copes with the scarcity of natural resources. Also see Steven Landsburg's superb discussion of population growth and resource use in chapter 13 of *Fair Play* (Free Press, 1997) along with many other fascinating applications of economics.

Air Bags (Chapter Three)

Information about the danger of air bags to children and small adults can be found at the National Highway Traffic Safety Administration (NHTSA) web site: http://www.nhtsa.gov/people/injury/airbags/airbag2/intro/alert1.htm. The challenges of installing an on-off switch for air bags can be found at http://www.nhtsa.gov/airbags/. Here is an excerpt from that web site dealing with some of those problems:

The National Highway Traffic Safety Administration (NHTSA) published a final rule on November 21, 1997 that sets forth a process allowing automobile dealers and repair businesses to install air bag on-off switches in the vehicles of certain, at-risk individuals. The process first requires that an individual submit an air bag on-off switch authorization request to NHTSA. Once the request has been authorized, NHTSA sends a letter to the individual which is then taken to a dealer or repair business. This letter has a tear-off portion which the dealer or repair business sends to NHTSA once the switch has been installed.

As of June 1, 1998, over 30,000 switch requests have been authorized by NHTSA. Only 1,000 of the dealer/repair business forms have been returned to NHTSA. Because of the disparity in these numbers, and because of numerous letters from vehicle owners who are searching for someone to install a switch, NHTSA has decided to publish on its web site a list of dealers and repair businesses willing to install switches. The agency would be pleased to add companies that would like to be added to this list.

The text goes on to try and reassure dealers and repair shops about the low probability of a lawsuit from installing an on-off switch.

Sam quotes a cost of $500 to install the on-off option. That was taken from a phone conversation on February 25, 2000 with an employee at a repair shop in San Jose, California, the Electric Battery Station, who said the cost of installation for most cars ranged from $475–$525. In St. Louis, I found one shop with a fee of $895.

Teacher Salaries (Chapter Five)

The American Federation of Teachers estimates that in 1999, the average salary for beginning teachers in Washington, D.C. with a BA was $30,000. Laura is at a private school, which tend to pay a little bit less, but she is at an elite private school, which would tend to boost the number. So I have put Laura's salary at $26,000.

Union Membership (Chapter Five)

In 1999, 9.4 percent of private employees were union members and 10.2 percent were represented by unions. The source is the U.S. Department of Labor, Bureau of Labor Statistics (BLS). I wish to thank Tom Beers of the BLS for this information.

Minimum Wage Jobs (Chapter Five)

In 1999, 4.6 percent of workers who were paid hourly earned at or below the minimum wage. For all workers, the proportion is presumably much lower. This figure is taken from the Bureau of Labor Statistics taken from the Current Population Survey. Again, I thank Tom Beers of the BLS for this information.

Morality and the Marketplace (Chapter Seven)

An insightful discussion of the view that good people are successful in business can be found in John Mueller's witty *Capitalism, Democracy, and Ralph's Pretty Good Grocery* (Princeton University Press, 1999). One example of Mueller's is how P. T. Barnum succeeded by treating the circus customer much better than his competitors did. Barnum's passion for honesty and customer service can be seen in his book, *The Art of Money-Getting* (Applewood Books, 1999). Incidentally, he never said "There's a sucker born every minute."

A nineteenth-century British version of the profitability of virtue and the morality of the market place can be found in Edwin Chadwick's "Opening Address of the President of Section F (Economic Science and Statistics) of the British Association for the Advancement of Science, at the Thirty-Second Meeting, at Cambridge, in October, 1862," *Journal of the Statistical Society of London* (December, 1862), now the *Journal of the Royal Statistical Society*. Chadwick says:

> Now, I had the pleasure of the acquaintance of perhaps the most wealthy and successful merchant of the last half-century . . . the later Mr. James Morrison, who assured me that the leading principles to which he owed his success in life, and which he vindicated as sound elements of economic science, were: always to consult the interests of the consumer, and not, as is the common maxim, to buy cheap and sell dear, but to sell cheap as well as to buy cheap; it being in his interest to widen the area of consumption, and to sell quickly and to the many . . . always to tell the truth, to have no shams; a rule he confessed he found it most difficult to get his common sellers to adhere to in its integrity, yet most important for success, it being to his interest as a merchant that any ship captain might come into his warehouse and fill his ships with goods of which he had no technical knowledge, but of which he well knew that only a small profit was charged upon a close ready-money purchasing price, and that go where he would he would find nothing cheaper. . . .

Sam Walton couldn't have said it better. The entire article can be found at http://www.jstor.org/cgi-bin/jstor/listjournal.

Economy as Ecosystem (Chapter Seven)

The economy as ecosystem and the spontaneous order produced by the marketplace without control has its roots in the work of Hayek and goes back to Adam Smith if not earlier. For a creative treatment of the topic see Michael Rothschild's *Bionomics: Economy as Ecosystem* (Henry Holt, reissue edition, 1995). A superb, brief talk by Rothschild on public policy using the ecosystem metaphor is available on audiotape through the Mercatus Center at George Mason University. The title is "From Mechanic to Gardener: Changing Roles in the Information Economy," Tape #10766.

Jane Jacobs uses the ecosystem metaphor to explore urban development in interesting ways in *The Nature of Economies* (Modern Library, 2000). Tom Petzinger's *The New Pioneers* (Free Press, 1999) uses the metaphor to tell fascinating stories about the explosion of innovation in the new economy. Also see Virginia Postrel's *The Future and Its Enemies* (Free Press, 1998) for a defense of an unplanned future.

Eggs, Inflation, and the Standard of Living (Chapter Seven)

The data on teacher's salaries in 1900 is taken from the *Historical Statistics of the United States. Colonial Times to 1970* (U.S. Department of Commerce, Bicentennial Edition, 1975), Series D 739-764, on p. 167. The price of eggs in 1900 is found there also in Series E 187-202 on p. 213. For an excellent overview of how America's standard of living has been transformed in the twentieth century, see Stanley Lebergott's *Pursuing Happiness* (Princeton University Press, 1993) and *Myths of the Rich and Poor: Why We're Better Off Than We Think* (Basic Books, 2000) by Michael Cox and Richard Alm.

Slide Rules (Chapter Seven)

I once read about a Keuffel and Esser study in 1967 of the year 2067 that failed to foresee the advent of calculators. The study may be apocryphal—if any reader knows of the study, please contact me.

Merck's Philosophy (Chapter Seven)

George W. Merck, the son of Merck's founder and the company's president from 1925–1950, said: "We try to remember that medicine is for the patient. We try never to forget that medicine is for the people. It is not for the profits. The profits follow, and if we have remembered that, they have never failed to appear. The better we have remembered that, the larger they have been." The quote is from a 1950 address at the Medical College of Virginia. I want to thank Gwendolyn Fisher at Merck for tracking down the source and author of the quote. She has told me that the quote is printed in every edition of the employee newsletter and that the current CEO, Raymond Gilmartin, often uses the quote in his speeches.

The Bagel Baker (Chapter Seven)

The example of the bagel baker is adapted from examples of Bastiat and Walter Williams. It has been helped by conversations with David Henderson and Dwight Lee. I want to thank Dwight for the following quotation from Dennis Robertson's *Economic Commentaries* (Staples Press Limited, 1954), p. 154:

What does the economist economize? "'Tis love, 'tis love," said the Duchess, "that makes the world go round." "Somebody said," whispered Alice, "that it's done by everybody minding their own business." "Ah well," replied the Duchess, "it means very much the same thing." ... But if we economists mind our own business and do that business well, we can, I believe, contribute mightily to the economizing, that is the full but thrifty utilization, of that scarce resource Love—which *we* know, just as well as anybody else, to be the most precious thing in the world.

The Social Responsibility of Business (Chapter Eleven)

Andrew refers to Sam's faith in the marketplace as some kind of "Milton Friedman thing." See Milton Friedman, "The Social Responsibility of Business Is to Increase Its Profits," *New York Times Magazine*, September

13, 1970. This brief and eloquent discussion of corporate responsibility covers some of the themes in this book.

The Dream Machine (Chapter Thirteen)
The Dream Machine is found in Robert Nozick's mind-expanding *Anarchy, State, and Utopia* (Basic Books, 1977).

The Fisherman in Heaven (Chapter Fifteen)
I don't know where I first heard this story. If anyone knows a source, please contact me.

Private Charity and Public Welfare (Chapter Fifteen)
Most of Sam's discussion of the impact of federal welfare spending during the Great Depression on private charity and the state of private charity today is taken from my article in the *Journal of Political Economy* (1984, vol. 92, no. 1), "A Positive Model of Private Charity and Public Transfers." I have also benefited from conversations with Glen Koenen, head of Circle of Concern, a St. Louis charity.

Maimonides' eight levels of charity can be found in his *Mishne Torah, Zeraim,* Laws of Gifts to the Poor, chapter 10, laws 7–14. The levels, from highest to lowest are as follows:

1. To give a gift, loan, job, or create a partnership that makes the needy person self-sufficient.
2. Neither giver nor the receiver knows the identity of the other.
3. The giver knows the identity of the receiver, but the receiver does not know the identity of the giver.
4. The receiver knows the identity of the giver but the giver does not know the identity of the receiver.
5. The giver gives without being asked.

6. The giver gives only after being asked, but gives a fitting amount.

7. The giver gives less than a fitting amount, but gives cheerfully.

8. The giver gives grudgingly.

I wish to thank Rabbi Chona Muser for help in studying and translating this text.

Private Vouchers (Chapter Fifteen)

The Children's Scholarship Fund, one of a number of private voucher programs, was started in 1998 with a gift of $100 million from Ted Forstmann and John Walton. Over one million children applied for the initial 40,000 scholarships. See *U.S. News and World Report*, April 26, 1999: http://www.usnews.com/usnews/issue/990426/26vouc.htm, or the *Philanthropy News Digest*, volume 5, issue 16, April 21, 1999: http://fdncenter.org/pnd/19990421/002646.html.

Moving Factories to Mexico (Chapter Seventeen)

For further discussion of the impact of moving American production over-seas and other issues of globalization, see my book on international trade and trade policy, *The Choice: A Fable of Free Trade and Protectionism* (Prentice Hall, revised edition, 2000).

Malden Mills (Chapter Seventeen)

Background for the discussion of Malden Mills was taken from various news accounts and a phone conversation on February 29, 2000 with Jeanne Wallace, Director of External Relations for Malden Mills.

Labor Market Transformation (Chapter Seventeen)

Agricultural employment in 1900 was 41 percent of total employment. See *Historical Statistics of the United States: Colonial Times to 1970* (U.S. Department of Commerce, bicentennial edition, 1975), series D 1-10, p. 126. Agricultural employment in 1999 was 2.5 percent of total employment (*Economic Report of the President*, 2000, table B-33, p. 146). Manufacturing employment as a percentage of total nonagricultural employment fell from 34 percent in 1950 to 14 percent in 1999 (*Economic Report of the President*, 2000B-44, p. 358).

Australian Prisoners (Chapter Eighteen)

Most of Sam's discussion of the impact of federal welfare spending during Background for the account given in the text was taken from Charles Bateson's *The Convict Ships* (Brown, Son & Ferguson, 1959, Glasgow, Scotland). Bateson (p. 6) describes the incentives when captains were paid on a per capita basis, regardless of how many convicts survived the trip: "Indeed, dead convicts were more profitable than the living, since every prisoner who died on the passage represented a saving in the expenditure on provisions."

Paying captains according to how many convicts survived the trip was an early innovation that reduced mortality dramatically. According to Bateson's account, based on reviews of the log-books and other material, the first 26 ships that carried convicts to Australia between 1790 and 1792 under private contract had a combined mortality rate of 498 out of 4082 convicts conveyed, or 12 percent, with a high on one ship, the Neptune, of 37 percent (158 out of 424). In 1793, three ships embarked for Australia under the new system of paying the contractors according to how many convicts got off the boat. Of the 422 convicts transported, only one died en route.

Bateson seems to suggest (p. 20) that this innovation was only used sporadically. He attributes the low mortality rates in the period after 1820 to the regular presence of naval surgeons on the later voyages, but it appears that they too had an economic incentive (pp. 20, 45), namely, the payment of bonuses based on the health and survival of the prisoners. And while Bateson uses selective numbers (p. 253) to make the case for the importance of the surgeons' supervision, he does say that "Curiously enough, there was, after 1801, an improvement in the conditions in the convict ships." Perhaps it was not so curious: earlier on the same page he says "... after 1800 the bonuses [paid to the surgeons, among others] were paid in most instances and ultimately in all."

Edwin Chadwick, from the same speech quoted above on page xxx, sums up the economics of the convict situation (though his numbers differ a bit from Bateson's):

At first, instances occurred of as many as one-half being thrown overboard during the passage. Humanity was appealed to in vain, and the sufferings and loss were held to in the natural and unavoidable order of things until the economic principle was applied of contracting for results. Instead of contracts being made for the numbers embarked, payment was contracted for only each person landed alive. . . . The result was a reduction in the sickness and mortality amongst persons of bad lives to about one and one half per cent. I took some pains to get the principle applied to the protection of pauper emigrants, and with the like satisfactory result. In these cases economy beat sentiment and benevolence. It evoked unwonted care for the passengers and secured to every poor man who died at least one sincere mourner.

I learned about the story of the Australian prisoners from Dwight Lee and from Robert Ekelund and Robert Hébert's book, *A History of Economic Theory and Method* (McGraw-Hill, 1983). I'm grateful to Ekelund and Hébert for their citation of Chadwick's delightful 1862 address. Unfortunately, it appears that contrary to their account, Chadwick did not come up with the inventive scheme to improve the lot of Australian-bound convicts, but rather applied it to the case of pauper emigration, presumably a part of Poor Law legislation.

Scrubbers, Sulfur Dioxide, and Tradeable Permits (Chapter Eighteen)

For an analysis of the tradeable permits portion of the Clean Air Act, see "An Interim Evaluation of Sulfur Dioxide Emissions Trading," by Richard Schmalensee, Paul L. Joskow, A. Denny Ellerman, Juan Pablo Montero, and Elizabeth Bailey, and "What Can We Learn from the Grand Policy Experiment? Lessons from SO2 Allowance Trading," by Robert Stavins in the *Journal of Economic Perspectives*, summer 1998, volume 12, no. 3.

Elephants in Africa (Chapter Eighteen)

Most news accounts of the African elephant population say that it fell from 1.2 million in 1980 to around 600,000 by the end of the decade. I have seen various estimates of the rise in Zimbabwe's population over various time periods, but no one seems to dispute that it has climbed dramatically since individuals and villages have been given a stake in elephant survival. Zimbabwe began such a program with the Parks and Wildlife Act of 1975 followed in the 1980s by Operation Windfall and CAMPFIRE (Communal Areas Management Programme for Indigenous Resources, www.campfire-zimbabwe.org).

Zimbabwe's elephant populations appear to have been 30,000–40,000 in the 1970s, 50,000 by the end of the 1980s, and 60,000–70,000 presently. Opponents of the CAMPFIRE program prefer continuing the ban on the ivory trade that was put in place in 1989 as the best means to reduce poaching. It is unclear whether the successes of the ivory ban (which appear to have stabilized or increased the elephant population outside of Zimbabwe) can be sustained given the costs of fighting poaching.

Zimbabwe currently allows about 200 elephants to be hunted each year out of a population of 60,000–70,000. Kenya, which was thought to have lost 80 percent of its elephants in the 1980s, lost 17 elephants to poachers on a single day in 1989.

These numbers and background for the discussion in the text can be found in publications from the World Wildlife Fund for Nature (WWF) at their web site: http://www.panda.org/resources/publications/species/, from *Elephants and Ivory: Lessons from the Trade Ban* (Institute of Economic Affairs, 1994), and from various reports including Kevin Hill, "Zimbabwe's Wildlife Conservation Regime: Rural Farmers and the State," *Human Ecology* (volume 19, 1991); "Can 'CAMPFIRE' Save the Elephant?" report by Cheri Sugal, *Environmental News Network*, April 1997; "Economics, Politics, and Controversy Over African Elephant Conservation," by Randy Simmons and Urs Kreuter, in *Elephants and Whales: Resources for Whom* (Gordon and Breach Science Publishers, 1994), edited by Milton M. R. Freeman and Urs P. Kreuter; and *Wildlife in the Marketplace* (Rowman and Littlefield, 1995), edited by Terry Anderson and Peter Hill. I have also benefited from conversations with Randy Simmons of Utah State University and Urs Kreuter of Texas A&M University.

A negative view of the incentives provided by the CAMPFIRE program and its effectiveness can be found in "CAMPFIRE: A Close Look at the Costs and Consequences" (Humane Society of the United States, April 1997).

The Elks of Yellowstone (Chapter Eighteen)

The discussion of the elk, wolf, and beaver is taken from *Playing God in Yellowstone* by Alston Chase; *The Yellowstone Primer: Land and Resource Management in the Greater Yellowstone Ecosystem,* edited by John Baden and Donald Leal (Pacific Research Institute for Public Policy, 1990); *Yellowstone: Ecological Malpractice,* by Charles E. Kay, PERC report vol. 15, No. 2, June 1997; and Robert Beschta's report to the Natural Resources Council Committee on Ungulate Management in Yellowstone National Park. In addition to the above reading, I have benefited from conversations with John Baden of the Foundation for Research on Economics and the Environment (FREE), Robert Beschta of Oregon State University, Pete Geddes of FREE, and Charles Kay of Utah State University.

Yellowstone Park officials deny there is an elk problem or that the Yellowstone ecosystem has been mismanaged. They dispute the claims of degradation of willow and aspen. Some of the official Park views can be found at http://www.nps.gov/yell/nature/index.htm.

In recent years, the National Park Service has followed a policy of "natural regulation," which in practice means leaving nature to take its own course in some areas (such as leaving the elk population unchecked) while allowing massive human intervention in others (removal of predators, millions of tourists, etc.). An alternative philosophy is outlined in Daniel Botkin's *Discordant Harmonies* (Oxford University Press, 1990).

Russell Roberts (Roberts@csab.wustl.edu) is the John M. Olin Senior Fellow at the Murray Weidenbaum Center on the Economy, Government, and Public Policy at Washington University in St. Louis. His first book, *The Choice: A Fable of Free Trade and Protectionism* (Prentice Hall, 1994; updated and revised edition, 2000) was named one of the top business books of the year by *Business Week* and the *Financial Times.* He is currently working on a web-based introduction to economics using graphs and data. In addition to teaching at Washington University in St. Louis, he has taught at UCLA, Stanford and the University of Rochester. He received his B.A. in economics from the University of North Carolina and his Ph.D. in economics from the University of Chicago.